DATE DUE

DEMCO 38-296

"WHAT DID YOU LEARN IN SCHOOL TODAY?"

A Parent's Guide For Evaluating Your Child's School

Harlow G. Unger

Facts On File
New York • Oxford

"WHAT DID YOU LEARN IN SCHOOL TODAY?"
A Parent's Guide for Evaluating Your Child's School

Copyright © 1991 by Harlow G. Unger

Facts On File, Inc.
460 Park Avenue South
New York NY 10016
USA

Facts On File Limited
Collins Street
Oxford OX4 1XJ
United Kingdom

Library of Congress Cataloging-in-Publication Data
Unger, Harlow G., 1931–
    What did you learn in school today? : a parent's guide for evaluating your child's school / Harlow G. Unger.
        p.   cm.
    Includes index.
    ISBN 0-8160-2510-X
    1. Education—United States—Evaluation—Handbooks, manuals, etc.
    2. Schools—United States—Evaluation—Handbooks, manuals, etc.
    3. Education—United States—Parent participation—Handbooks, manuals, etc.   I. Title.
    LA217.2.U54   1991
    370.19'3—dc20   90-21724

British CIP data available on request from Facts On File.

Facts On File books are available at special discounts when purchased in bulk quantities for businesses, associations, institutions or sales promotions. Please contact the Special Sales Department of our New York office at 212/683-2244 (dial 800/322-8755 except in NY, AK or HI).

Text design by Ron Monteleone
Jacket design by Ed Atkeson/Berg Design
Composition by the Maple-Vail Book Manufacturing Group
Manufactured by the Maple-Vail Book Manufacturing Group
Printed in the United States of America

10 9 8 7 6 5 4 3 2 1

This book is printed on acid-free paper.

TO THE GREAT TEACHERS IN MY LIFE

MY PARENTS
Beatrice R. Unger
&
Lester J. Unger, M.D.

MY MENTORS
Jacques Grosbois
Hugh and Doris Newnham
Del MacKenzie

TABLE OF CONTENTS

ACKNOWLEDGMENTS

The author wishes to express special thanks to those whose help made this book possible: Dr. Susan K. Nicklas, Commission on Elementary Schools, Middle States Association of Colleges and Schools, Philadelphia, Pa.; Dr. George H. Brown, Office of Educational Research and Improvement, United States Department of Education, Washington, D.C.; Dr. Peter Gibbon, Headmaster, Hackley School, Tarrytown, N.Y.; Mrs. Kathleen P. Potier, Mannheim Township High School, Neffsville, Pa.; Mr. Ronald D. Potier, Director of Admissions, Elizabethtown College, Elizabethtown, Pa.; Ms. Deborah Brody, Associate Editor, Harper-Collins Publishers; Mr. Neal Maillet and Ms. Kathy Ishizuka, Project Editors, Facts On File Publications; and Ms. Paula Diamond, The Paula Diamond Agency.

If a nation expects to be ignorant and free, in a state of civilization, it expects what never was and never will be.
                    —Thomas Jefferson

Knowledge will forever govern ignorance: And a people who mean to be their own Governors, must arm themselves with the power which knowledge gives.
                    —James Madison

PART I

THE SEARCH FOR QUALITY

CHAPTER 1

WHO'S TEACHING YOUR KIDS?

When you ask your children, "What did you learn in school today?", do you know what the answer should be?

You know, of course, that your children are studying third grade reading, writing and arithmetic—or high school English, chemistry and American history. But do you know whether they're learning as much reading, writing and arithmetic as they should—as much as other American kids their age? In other words, are you certain your children are getting the educational equipment to handle advanced school work and, eventually, the requirements of college and a good job?

And what do you know about your children's teachers and school principal? Do you know where they went to school and what they studied or anything else about their qualifications, such as whether they have graduate degrees or even undergraduate degrees in the courses they're teaching? Diplomas on pediatricians' office walls assure us of their training, knowledge and authority, but classroom walls give us no such assurances about our children's teachers. George Washington's silent portrait says nothing about a teacher's professional competence, training or educational background. There is not even any evidence that the teacher studied the subject matter being taught.

And what about your children's schools? The best teachers cannot do their jobs properly if the schools in which they work do not provide adequate teaching materials and the right curriculum. Are your children's schools competitive? Are they offering as much knowledge and as many educational opportunities as other American schools or schools in other countries, such as Canada, Britain, Germany or Japan? In many communities, 25% or more of the children who graduate from high school are too illiterate to hold the most menial jobs, let alone go on to college. According to one U.S. government study, more than half the 17-year-olds in America cannot read or write adequately. In many schools, learning to cook and drive counts as much toward a high school diploma as English and math—despite endless studies proving that most high school vocational courses not only teach insufficient and obsolete job skills, they leave students inadequately trained academically. In other words, the time spent in cooking classes is usually wasted because such classes not only fail to teach students to cook professionally, they deprive students of the opportunity to learn how to read, write and calculate at an adult level. One-quarter of the credits earned by general-track high school students in the United States are for physical and health education, work outside the school, remedial courses and "personal service and development" courses—leaving millions of high school graduates semiliterate.

Even schools in affluent suburbs produce scores of children incapable of writing an intelligible letter or communicating thoughts with words more complex than "Like, ya know . . . well, like . . . it was cool, you know?" Such gibberish is not just indicative of a "phase" that children will outgrow. It is a reflection of their education. The U.S. Department of Education found that nearly 90% of U.S. 13-year-olds are "not adept at reading and are unable to understand complex information," and it found that "students at all grade levels are deficient in higher order thinking skills."

Can the principal of your children's school and the school board in your community assure you this won't happen to your children?

And who are the members of the school board? Are they university graduates? High school graduates? What knowledge, training and professional backgrounds do they have in education? Do they have the professional competence to determine what your child should and should not study?

If you can't answer any or all of these questions, you're no different from the majority of American parents. Most of us without professional training find it difficult to evaluate professional competence. In picking a doctor, we often follow the recommendations of nonprofessional friends and relatives because we know we can rely on the tough national training standards of American medical schools to screen out most incompetents. Medical schools usually won't accept students with poor college grades or poor scores on medical school entrance examinations, and they do not award M.D.s to academically incompetent students.

Because that's usually true in other American professions, most parents assume it's true in education. The most concerned, loving parents willingly and routinely entrust the minds and bodies of their children to their local schools, assuming that state education authorities and local school boards are made up of people knowledgeable about education and that local schools are under the control and direction of professional educators. Unfortunately, that can be a dangerous assumption, because the profession of education has no national standards of competency and is the only profession governed by nonprofessionals.

Teachers and school administrators need no minimum college grades or standardized test scores to teach a particular subject or run a school. Almost anyone can be a teacher. Most "come from the lower half of their college classes," according to the Carnegie Foundation for the Advancement of Teaching. What's more, they usually don't even need degrees in the subjects they teach. They can major in modern dance at college and go on to teach history or math or anything else. A U.S. government study in 1983, found that one-half of the math, science and English teachers hired at the time were not qualified to teach those subjects. Those teachers are now presiding in school classrooms across the United States and have almost 10 years' tenure. The study also found that less than one-third of U.S. public high school physics courses are taught by qualified teachers. Twenty percent of American teachers admit they have been assigned to teach subjects they are not qualified to teach.

The standards are even lower—indeed nonexistent—for school board members, who often determine what our children must learn. They need no background or training in education. They don't have to be college or high school graduates—or even pass literacy tests—to serve on a school board and decide who will teach our children and what our children will have to study. Many school boards actually refuse to share policy-making powers with educators. More than half the teachers in U.S. public schools have no say in setting standards for student promotions or student behavior. Nearly 40% of teachers have almost no say in determining the curriculum they teach. In 21 states, political appointees in state capitals dictate the textbooks—and sometimes even the lesson plans—every teacher must use in every public school class.

Making matters worse is the lack of national standards in education. Each state and often each school district has different standards—usually set by politicians, not educators. Some states have strict standards, but some have almost none and leave all standards-setting to local school boards.

The result for U.S. elementary, middle and high schools is an educational hodgepodge that permits any child—your child—to graduate from one high school ready for Harvard or graduate from another an educational cripple, unable to read, write or calculate adequately to attend college or even hold a job.

"If an unfriendly foreign power had attempted to impose on America the mediocre educational performance that exists today," the National Commission on Excellence in Education warned, "we might well have viewed it as an act of war."

The danger for us as parents is that, for the first time in U.S. history, we can no longer expect schools automatically to give our children an education as good or better than we had. Now that doesn't mean there aren't any great schools or great teachers. There are—all across the United States. The problem is to identify them, and that's why, if you're among the millions of families moving to a new community this year or if your children are approaching kindergarten age, it's vital to their educational health to determine the quality of local schools and teachers. Even if your children are already enrolled in school, failure to evaluate school quality could condemn them to substandard education and lost college and career opportunities.

Many parents don't realize they have many choices in educating their children—which is why I've written this book: to give you a set of professional standards for making those choices wisely. The rest of Part I will show you how to evaluate education in each state and school district and how to evaluate individual schools, both private and public, as well as their principals and faculties. The end of each chapter has a checklist that summarizes the basic questions you'll need answered to evaluate local education. A set of detailed "Report Cards" in Part II will take you step-by-step through an in-depth evaluation of every aspect of schooling and compare the quality of schools you see with national averages.

Part III—"The Academic Curriculum"—will show you exactly what teachers should be teaching and what your children should be learning in every subject and every grade from kindergarten through high school. It will let you compare the quality of any school's curriculum with a range of minimum accepted standards recommended by the National Commission on Excellence in Education and derived from a U.S. Department of Education "Curriculum for American Students" and from curricula at leading U.S. public and private schools accredited by one of the six regional accreditation associations.

Those associations were established over the past century by educators to provide minimum standards for both public and private primary, middle and secondary schools. Unfortunately, accreditation is voluntary in most areas, and sometimes fewer than 10% of public schools seek accreditation or attempt to meet the standards required for accreditation. Chapter 2 explains accreditation and what it means to you as a parent selecting a school for your children. You'll also find some alternative courses of action when you think you're trapped in an area of substandard schools.

Your children—and all children in the United States—have a fundamental right to obtain an education that will guarantee their ability to go to college if they choose, to work productively and to govern themselves and their communities intelligently. It's up to us, as parents, to assure them of those rights by seeing that they have professionally competent teachers and school administrators and that they are studying the right materials. I hope the following pages will help you assure your children of those rights.

A FEW WORDS OF CAUTION

No school is perfect for every child at every age. So it's important to continue to update your school evaluation each year as your children move from grade to grade and from teacher to teacher. It's also important to evaluate each new administrator who takes charge of your children's schools and each new candidate for the school board.

Remember, too, that no school can properly educate your children without your full cooperation as a parent. During the first years of your children's lives, you are their only teacher, and you'll remain their most important teacher well into, and perhaps even beyond, their teen years.

Parents who read no books cannot expect schools to make their children enthusiastic readers, and parents who watch television every moment of every evening cannot expect their children to prefer spending their own evenings doing homework. Regardless of the quality of your children's schools and teachers, your children's academic performance will ultimately reflect their intellectual life at home.

Educators across the United States are calling for parents to be more involved in their children's education. This is not a call for parents to interfere in the educational process at school or to impose their personal political, religious or moral beliefs on local school systems. It *is* a call for parents to impose behavioral controls on their children at home. It is a call for parents to fill their homes with books and to read to their children when they're young, to monitor their homework and to support school and teacher demands for greater academic effort by their children. It is a call to limit family (and children's) TV viewing and to see that children get enough sleep and a proper diet. It is a call to enrich your children's cultural lives and supplement their education by taking them to museums and plays and other cultural attractions—and not pull them out of school for frivolous activities such as a sports event or a ski vacation. It's a call not to excuse poor school performance simply because your children contend their school work is too difficult—though they clearly have the ability to learn. It's a call to make them work harder when they do poorly. And it's a call to monitor carefully your children's activities in and out of school and to monitor your children's curriculum and insure that they take courses that fulfill the demands of college and the workplace.

One other word of caution: This book is designed as an evaluative tool for making wise educational choices for your children—not as a weapon to do battle with your children's teachers and school administrators. Your children will be the only losers in such a struggle. Regardless of your interest in raising educational standards in your community, that campaign must be waged on another front with soldiers other than your own children. There is not enough time in their educational lives to wage social wars. Let them do that as adults once they are armed with a good education. For now, every minute of their time must be preciously reserved for formal learning.

By all means, make friendly suggestions to try to improve your children's schools. If enough parents feel as you do, perhaps your school will change for the better. But institutional change comes slowly, and, in most cases, the changes you suggest will come too late to affect your children's education.

So, for now, concentrate on careful evaluation as the most effective method of obtaining the best possible education for your children.

WHAT'S A "GOOD" SCHOOL?

Before we start, let me explain a few terms that might be misunderstood. By an "average" school, I mean one that meets the standards of, and is accredited by, the six regional school accreditation associations listed at the end of Chapter 2. Any school that does not meet those standards is called "substandard," "below average" or "poor-quality." Unfortunately, the majority of U.S. public schools now fall into that category.

Elementary and middle schools called "good," "best" or "top-quality" are ones whose students consistently perform at or above grade level, as determined by objectively administered, standardized achievement tests. The "best" high schools are those whose students consistently score in the top 50% on the College Board Achievement Tests and Scholastic Aptitude Test and on other college admissions tests. The "best" high schools send 75% to 100% of their students to college or to effective career-education programs at community colleges and technical institutes. Three-quarters or more of their teachers have master's degrees or equivalent credentials in non-academic areas. They have been on the job at the same schools for 15 years or more and are almost never absent from their classes during the school year.

The qualities of the "best" schools will become clearer as you progress through the book. But just to give you a quick picture, the U.S. Department of Education funded several research projects to identify the most outstanding public elementary, middle and high schools in the United States and to determine what characteristics they all had in common. All had these characteristics:

- Clearly stated academic goals and a clearly defined core curriculum with few electives
- High expectations and academic standards for students, with students expected to adjust upward to high standards rather than standards ever being lowered to adjust to unwilling students. The result: More than 85% of students performed at or above grade level on standardized tests
- Concentration on learning during classtime, with no interruptions for administrative announcements and procedures
- Order and discipline, with emphasis on character development
- A pleasant, safe and professional work environment, where highly paid principals and teachers controlled academic planning
- Strong administrative leadership. Average tenure for principals was seven years. Almost 80% had served four or more years, and 35% had served nine or more years.
- Extensive student participation in student government, school extracurricular activities and community programs
- Strong school spirit, with average student *and* teacher attendance rates of 95% or more
- Strong community and parental support and involvement

The rest of Part I will explain each of these and many other qualities of "good" schools and show you how to measure them objectively and accurately in every school and every grade from kindergarten through high school.

Before beginning, let's clear up another term that confuses many parents, namely "middle school." Some communities continue to use the traditional primary-secondary school divisions, with primary, or elementary, school stretching from kindergarten through sixth grade, and secondary, or high, school covering seventh through twelfth grade education. After World War II, when high school student populations grew too large to house in one building, however, many communities built a third school—a junior high school, now called middle school—to absorb seventh and eighth graders. As local school populations expanded, especially during the baby boom years, the composition of such middle schools began stretching in all sorts of directions. Some incorporated seventh, eighth and ninth grades, others fifth, sixth, seventh and eighth, and even ninth—so that they sometimes had more grades than either elementary or high school. The combinations became—and remain—unpredictable from one area to the next. Whatever their composition, most good middle schools are now designed and staffed with trained specialists to meet the particular needs of young adolescents—children "in the middle," whose intellectual, physical and emotional needs differ substantially from preadolescents and high school teenagers.

With that explanation in mind, let's start evaluating elementary, middle and high schools for your children.

CHAPTER 2

EVALUATING STATE AND DISTRICT SCHOOL SYSTEMS

It's a good idea to get a sense of the educational climate of a state and school district before investing your child's academic future in an area. It's true that even a state or school district with generally poor education may host some exceptionally good schools; Chapters 3 through 6 will show you how to identify them. Some areas try to complement average or below-average public schools systems with so-called "magnet" schools designed to nurture the talents of the area's most gifted children. But even the best public schools can deteriorate quickly if a state, county or city government decides to cut spending on education. Moreover, it's difficult for most children to do their best in an environment in which good education is not held in high esteem by the entire community.

So if you're among the 15% to 20% of American families planning to move this year, it's important to evaluate the education system of the state and school district where your children will *attend* school *before* you move. Remember: in some areas your children may not attend schools near your new home if busing is required to achieve racial balance in local schools. It's not as difficult as it sounds to evaluate the education system of a state or school district. All you need are a few easy-to-understand statistics that you can use to compare education in any state or school district with national averages. Table 1 lists those statistics, and Table 2 rates each state against the national average on the basis of "A" for Above Average, "S" for Satisfactory (average) and "F" for Inferior (well below average). Use Table 2 as a quick guide to educational quality of each state school system. The statistics are updated every year and published by the U.S. Department of Education in its *Digest of Education Statistics,* which is available in most major public libraries or from the U.S. Government Printing Office in Washington, D.C.

Table 1

STATE EDUCATION STATISTICS

	Spending per pupil	School spending as % of all govt. spending	Actual average teacher salaries	Pupil–teacher ratio	Grad rate	Dropout rate
United States	$3,739	24.2%	$28,044	17.4	72.6%	27.4%
Alabama	2,308	20.7	23,320	18.7	74.1	25.9
Alaska	7,909	17.4	40,424	17.0	69.8	30.2
Arizona	4,012	25.2	27,388	18.2	66.6	33.4
Arkansas	2,777	28.3	20,340	15.7	78.7	21.3
California	3,689	20.6	33,159	22.7	68.5	31.5
Colorado	4,053	25.7	28,851	17.8	76.5	23.5
Connecticut	4,650	23.7	33,487	13.1	82.2	17.8
Delaware	3,974	21.6	29,575	16.4	69.8	30.2
District of Columbia	5,681	14.5	34,705	13.3	60.2	39.8
Florida	3,902	24.1	25,198	17.1	63.0	37.0
Georgia	3,401	26.5	26,177	18.5	63.4	36.6
Hawaii	2,843	17.3	28,785	21.1	81.7	18.3
Idaho	2,461	24.6	22,242	20.6	76.8	23.2
Illinois	3,323	23.5	29,663	17.1	78.2	21.8
Indiana	3,264	27.4	27,386	17.8	78.1	21.9
Iowa	3,552	24.7	24,867	15.8	86.9	13.1
Kansas	3,606	26.1	24,647	15.2	82.7	17.3
Kentucky	2,554	22.0	24,274	17.8	69.1	30.9
Louisiana	2,425	20.1	21,209	18.2	61.6	38.4
Maine	3,723	25.2	23,425	14.6	77.7	22.3
Maryland	3,961	23.3	30,933	16.8	76.1	23.9
Massachusetts	4,316	20.8	30,019	13.7	69.9	30.1
Michigan	4,075	25.2	32,926	19.8	72.9	27.1
Minnesota	4,326	23.0	29,900	17.0	89.5	10.5
Mississippi	2,538	24.8	20,669	18.4	67.5	32.5
Missouri	3,239	27.7	24,703	15.9	75.5	24.5
Montana	3,975	27.9	23,796	15.8	84.7	15.3
Nebraska	3,574	26.0	23,246	15.0	85.9	14.1
Nevada	3,533	21.0	27,600	20.3	73.0	27.0
New Hampshire	3,773	27.6	24,091	16.2	77.2	22.8
New Jersey	4,912	25.1	30,720	13.6	80.4	19.6
New Mexico	3,282	24.2	24,351	18.5	73.4	26.6
New York	5,429	22.2	34,500	14.9	66.3	33.7
North Carolina	3,328	26.8	24,900	17.5	68.0	32.0
North Dakota	3,366	22.6	21,660	15.4	88.3	11.7

	Spending per pupil	School spending as % of all govt. spending	Actual average teacher salaries	Pupil–teacher ratio	Grad rate	Dropout rate
Ohio	3,674	26.9	27,606	17.6	76.4	23.6
Oklahoma	2,990	25.4	22,006	16.5	74.0	26.0
Oregon	4,347	26.3	28,060	18.4	71.7	28.3
Pennsylvania	4,077	27.8	29,174	15.9	81.1	18.9
Rhode Island	3,957	21.4	32,858	14.6	70.5	29.5
South Carolina	3,159	27.4	24,241	17.2	65.2	34.8
South Dakota	3,121	26.0	19,750	15.4	86.7	13.3
Tennessee	2,527	21.2	23,785	19.3	68.6	31.4
Texas	3,348	28.3	26,655	17.5	64.9	35.1
Utah	2,493	26.3	22,621	24.5	81.3	18.7
Vermont	4,218	26.1	23,397	13.6	81.2	18.8
Virginia	4,046	26.5	27,436	16.1	74.6	25.4
Washington	4,103	25.9	28,116	20.4	78.0	22.0
West Virginia	3,258	27.7	21,736	15.1	76.8	23.2
Wisconsin	4,168	26.7	28,998	16.0	83.3	16.7
Wyoming	5,265	26.2	27,260	14.6	97.5	2.5

Source: *Digest of Education Statistics 1990*, National Center for Education Statistics, U.S. Department of Education, Washington, D.C.

The key figures that reflect the quality of a state's public school system are:

- *Spending per pupil.* The average for the United States was about $3,739 in 1989. It is unlikely that any state or school district that spent *less* than this average offered its children a quality education. Top-rated public and private day schools spend between $8,000 and $10,000 per pupil, and the finest boarding schools spend as much as $20,000 a year per student. But *above average* spending per pupil doesn't necessarily mean a superior education—although that's the figure politicians usually use to boast about their states' schools. There's no way, however, to know how much of the money spent for each student is for academics and how much is for sports, extracurricular activities, such as marching bands, or administrative services, such as transportation. So, spending per pupil, while important, is only a starting point in evaluating state education systems. It must be examined in conjunction with other figures, such as teacher salaries, which are a far better indication of how much the state spends on academics.
- *Spending on elementary and high school education as a percentage of all government spending in the state.* This figure tells you where the state

ranks education among its spending priorities. Once again, though, the figure can be meaningless unless examined in conjunction with all other statistics in this listing. Texas and Arkansas earmark 28.3% of all state and local spending for primary and secondary schools. That's the highest in the United States. But both rank well below the U.S. average in teacher pay. In fact, Arkansas ranked next to the bottom, which means its spending is not going into good teaching and academics.

- *Average annual teacher salaries.* For the United States, the average annual teacher salary was just over $28,000 at the beginning of 1990, with starting salaries averaging just under $20,000 a year. Low teacher pay almost always means low quality schools with high rates of teacher absenteeism and turnover. States that pay lower-than-average salaries have been plagued by teacher strikes, school closures and educational turmoil, all of which produce low quality education.

- *Pupil–teacher ratio.* For U.S. schools as a whole, the pupil–teacher ratio is a respectable 17.4. States or districts that cram 25 or 30 or more students in each classroom are not educating children—they're baby-sitting, and probably not doing that very well. Few teachers can maintain order, let alone teach effectively, in a classroom of 25 to 30 youngsters. Attendance-taking alone can consume 10 minutes of a 40-minute period. Top-ranked public and private schools have maximum pupil–teacher ratios of 10 to 15 students per teacher.

- *Graduation rates.* The percentage of students who graduate from high school in each state also tells you the percentage that did not graduate—i.e., the dropout rate. The national graduation rate in 1989 was only 72.6%, which puts the national dropout rate at a shamefully high 27.4%. High dropout rates are automatically an indication of poor quality schools with low student and teacher morale. Few students quit schools that make education exciting. As before, though, be careful about jumping to conclusions. Although all good schools have low dropout rates, not all schools with low dropout rates are necessarily good. A low dropout rate can also mean low academic standards that permit every student to pass and graduate.

- *Percentage of teachers reporting student behavior problems.* More than any other statistic, this reflects the quality of the public school environment your children would enter. Such factors as disruptive classroom behavior, student apathy, violence against students and against teachers and drug and alcohol abuse can all hurt your children's chances for a sound education. On an *average* day, according to a joint study by the American Medical Association and the National Association of State Boards of Education, 135,000 students bring guns to school. The study found that more than 1 million teenagers are regular users of drugs and that alcohol-related accidents are the leading cause of death among teenagers. So pay close attention to teacher reports of student behavior problems—and don't conclude that no problems exist in areas where teachers fail to report such problems. They may simply be ignoring them or be under orders to look the other way.

- *Percentage of teachers involved in making key educational decisions.* This rarely examined statistic is an indication of how much control professional educators have over schools in their state. In many states, education has become a battleground for special interest groups and politicians who know little—and care less—about quality education. To offer quality services, education, like all other professions, must be governed by knowledgeable professionals—trained educators. It is virtually impossible for children to respect and respond to a principal or to teachers who they know have no authority or decision-making responsibilities in the education process. If the adult community does not trust the professionalism of educators, their children won't either. So look to principal and teacher authority as one indication of the professionalism of education systems in each state.

Whether a state ranks above or below the national average on all or most of the seven qualities listed should be an important consideration in determining where you plan to educate your children. Table 2 compares educational indicators of each state with national averages and then, after a complex weighing procedure, assigns each state educational system a final grade. Remember that "S" for "Satisfactory" is no hallmark of quality given the poor conditions of American education in the average American public school. Remember also that states with average or below-average public school systems may have some outstanding individual schools. They will simply be fewer in number and perhaps harder to find. On the other hand, don't assume that every school in states with above-average systems of education will automatically be good. It's important to evaluate each school individually, and when you find a good one, keep searching. You may find a better one a few miles away in the next district.

State College Entrance Requirements

Another factor that can help you assess a state's education system is the selectivity of the public state university. Entrance requirements at

Table 2

COMPARATIVE REPORT CARD ON STATE EDUCATION

Symbols: A = Above Average Educ. System (more than 10% above U.S. average)
S = Satisfactory—within 10% of U.S. Average
F = Inferior Educ. System (more than 10% below U.S. average)

Plus (+) and minus (−) signs are used to show a state system that is better or worse than other states in each category.

	Spending per pupil (1)	School spending as % of all govt. spending	Average teacher salaries (1)	Pupil-teacher ratios	Graduation/ dropout rates	Teachers reporting serious student problems	Teacher input/ authority	FINAL GRADE
United States	S	S	S	S	S	S	S	S
Alabama	F−	F	F−	S	S	S	F	F−
Alaska	A+	F−	A+	S	S	S	S	(2)
Arizona	S	S	S	S	S	S	S	S
Arkansas	F−	A+	F−	S+	S	S	S	F
California	S	F	A+	F−	S	S	S	S−
Colorado	S	S	S	S	S	S	A	S
Connecticut	A+	S	A+	A+	A	S	S	A+
Delaware	S	F	S	S	S	F+	A	S
Dist. of Columbia	A+	F−	A+	A+	F−	?	?	(3)
Florida	S	S	S	S	F	F+	F	S−
Georgia	S	S+	S	S	F	S	F	S
Hawaii	F−	F−	S	F−	A	F−	A	F−
Idaho	F−	S	F−	F−	S	S	S	F−
Illinois	S	S	S	S	S	A	S	S
Indiana	F	A	S	S	S	S	A	S
Iowa	S	S	S	S+	A+	S−	A	S
Kansas	S	S	S	A	A	S	A	S
Kentucky	F−	S	F	S	S	S+	S	F
Louisiana	F−	F−	F−	S	F−	S−	F	F−
Maine	S	S	F−	A+	S	S+	A	S−
Maryland	S	S	S	S	S	S−	F	S
Massachusetts	A	F	S	A+	S	F	S	S
Michigan	A	S	A+	F	S	S	S	A
Minnesota	A+	S	S	S	A+	S	A	S+
Mississippi	F−	S	F−	S	S	S	S	F−
Missouri	F	A	F	S+	S	S	S	F
Montana	S	A+	F−	S+	A+	S+	A	S−
Nebraska	S	S	F	A	A+	F	A	S

Symbols: A = Above Average Educ. System (more than 10% above U.S. average)
S = Satisfactory—within 10% of U.S. Average
F = Inferior Educ. System (more than 10% below U.S. average)

Plus (+) and minus (−) signs are used to show a state system that is better or worse than other states in each category.

	Spending per pupil (1)	School spending as % of all govt. spending	Average teacher salaries (1)	Pupil-teacher ratios	Graduation/ dropout rates	Teachers reporting serious student problems	Teacher input/ authority	FINAL GRADE
Nevada	S	F	S	F−	S	S−	F	S−
New Hampshire	S	A	F−	S	S	S	A	S−
New Jersey	A+	S	S	A+	A	S+	S	S+
New Mexico	F	S	F	S	S	S−	A	F
New York	A+	S	A+	A	S	S−	S	A
North Carolina	S−	A	F+	S	S	F	S	F+
North Dakota	S	S	F−	A	A+	S+	A	S−
Ohio	S	A	S	S	S	S	A	S
Oklahoma	F−	S	F−	S	S	S−	A	F−
Oregon	A+	S+	S	S	S	S	A	S+
Pennsylvania	S	A	S	S	A	S	A	S
Rhode Island	S	F	A	A	S	S−	A	S
South Carolina	F	A	F	S	F	S	A	F
South Dakota	F−	S	F−	A	A+	S	A	F−
Tennessee	F−	F	F	F	S	S+	F	F−
Texas	S−	A+	S	S	F	S−	S	S−
Utah	F−	S+	F−	F−	A	S	S	F−
Vermont	S	S	F−	A+	A	S	A	S−
Virginia	S+	S+	S	S	S	S	S	S
Washington	S+	S	S	F−	S	S−	S	S
West Virginia	F	A	F−	A	S	S	F	F
Wisconsin	A	A	S	S	A	S	A	A
Wyoming	A+	S	S	A+	A+	S+	A	S+

(1) Spending per pupil and teacher salary rankings adjusted for regional cost-of-living differences.

(2) Alaska unranked because of difficulty in adjusting figures to high cost of living and determining quality of isolated schools.

(3) District of Columbia school system unranked because of its failure to report accurate figures to the Department of Education.

a state university usually reflect the quality of education of applicants from the state's public schools. Because of the failure of so many public schools to educate students adequately, half the state colleges in the United States have had to abandon *all* high school course requirements as a condition for admission, and most of the others admit 75% or more of their applicants. Don't be fooled by so-called "competency tests" that 40 states now require for high school diplomas. These barely measure literacy (see section on Academic Quality in Chapter 5), and most state colleges now have to offer remedial reading, remedial math and many of the basics that students should have studied in high school.

So, regardless of your child's age, it's worth looking through a *Barron's Profiles of American Colleges* (available at major libraries and book stores) to see the requirements of state colleges and universities in each area and where those colleges rank nationally. Many campuses in the California, New York and Michigan state university systems, for example, rank among the most selective colleges in the United States, while state university systems in many southern states, as well as Montana and Wyoming, rank among the least selective.

Another way to get an idea of the quality of education in a state is to listen to the news. Most major teacher strikes are reported by national television news, as are disputes over state spending on education. A state in constant turmoil over education is seldom a healthy place for children to go to school.

SCHOOL DISTRICTS

The same figures used to evaluate statewide education will also help you evaluate individual school districts. If spending per pupil, average teacher salaries, pupil-teacher ratios and graduation rates are below the national average shown in Table 1, the quality of education will also be below average. And if district figures are below state levels in a state that is below average, then the schools in that district will probably be terrible. The figures you'll need for each district (and school) should be available at the office of the superintendent of schools in the form of community and school "profiles" (Figure 3). By using those figures to fill in Report Card No. 1, you can quickly determine the quality of any school district.

A WORD ABOUT REPORT CARDS

Use the Report Cards in Part II of this book as a quick and easy way to jot down facts and figures and make evaluations of school districts and individual schools. There are eight report cards. The last four are for in-depth evaluations of individual schools. The first four are extremely short and easy to use and are designed to give you a few quick, preliminary evaluations of a school district (Report Card No. 1), its schools (Report Card No. 2) and its school board and superintendent (Report Card No. 3). Report Card No. 4 will show whether education is run by educators or noneducators. Together, the four report cards let you quickly eliminate substandard school districts and save the bother of long, tiring school visits. Take the report cards (or copies of them) with you to visits and interviews. They're selfexplanatory and easy to use, and they'll serve as handy lists of questions for you to ask as you proceed through the evaluation process.

THE SUPERINTENDENT'S OFFICE

You'll learn a great deal about the school district as you cross the threshold of the superintendent's office. Warm smiles and a friendly "May I help you" usually reflect a warm, cooperative relationship between school authorities and the community. Willingness to share facts and figures about school district performance—failures as well as triumphs—is further evidence of a strong educational system that has many accomplishments to its credit, is proud to display them and is constantly trying to improve. The profile of Lake Forest High School (Figure 1), an outstanding Illinois public school, is three pages long and gives prospective parents descriptions of school facilities, faculty and student body. It lists per-student spending ($8,099, or double the national average), student-teacher ratio (1:11, or 37.5% below the national average), and the fact that 85% of its faculty has master's degrees. Profiles of average schools are often only one page long and normally omit most of that data. A concerned parent should ask why.

Elementary school and middle school profiles are more limited than high school profiles. The former tend to list the curriculum, promotion and retention rates and a few achievement test scores which are often meaningless because of how they are put together and administered. High school profiles are more comprehensive. They should list student test scores on college entrance exams (Scholastic Aptitude Tests—both verbal and math scores—and the American College Testing Program scores in English, math, science and social studies). High school profiles should also give the school's graduation rate (and, therefore, dropout rate) and the percentages of graduating seniors who go to four-year public and private colleges, to two-year colleges, to work and into the military. Use Report Card No. 2 to compare school profiles with national averages and get quick preliminary evaluations that will save

Lake Forest High School, Lake Forest, Illinois   Community High School District No. 115

Who's Who at L.F.H.S.

Superintendent of Schools
  Dr. Robert H. Metcalf
Principal
  Marilyn A. Howell
Director of Pupil Personnel
  James Warfield
Counseling Staff Members
  Jacqueline Berkshire
  Gene Brooke
  Virginia Ditton
  Roger Hartmann
  James Jones
  Barbara Papp
  Patricia Sanborn
Athletic Director
  Terence J. Barton

1989 – 90 Statistical Profile of Lake Forest High School

School Address	
1285 North McKinley Road	
Lake Forest, Illinois 60045	
Telephone	
312-234-3600 (Please note: after	
November 11, 1989, the Area Code	
for Lake Forest will be 708)	
Total Enrollment	1,080
Seniors	270
Accreditation	North Central
Certified staff, F.T.E.	99.4
Certified staff-to-student ratio	1:11
Average tenure of faculty	15 years
Faculty holding master's	
degree or beyond	85%

School year	37 weeks
Annual per-pupil expenditure	
(1988 – 89)	$8,099
Library holdings	40,000 volumes
CEEB Code	142-520
Percent of graduates enrolling in	
four-year colleges	86%
Illinois State Scholars	76
Number of course titles in Lake Forest	
High School's curriculum	192
Number of Advanced Placement	
exams taken (1988 – 89)	161
Percent of Advanced Placement exam	
scores of three or above	82%

Lake Forest: Community and School

Lake Forest High School serves the residents of an Illinois community of 22,000. Located 30 miles north of Chicago, the community of Lake Forest is home to business and professional families who evidence strong demand for college preparatory education.

The community is exceptionally supportive of its institutions (which include the Lake Forest Symphony and Center Stage for the Performing Arts). For Lake Forest High School, this assistance takes the form of such items

as college scholarships, foreign exchange programs and the gift of an all-weather track from the parents of athletes.

The school was built in 1935 and is continually updated as needs change. The curriculum is extensive, and recent additions to school facilities include a Computer-Assisted Instruction Laboratory, construction of television retrieval carrels and the development of a library of 2,200 curriculum-related videotapes; the establishment of a reading labora-

tory; and the acquisition of a nature preserve which serves as an outdoor laboratory for the biology department.

The average tenure of faculty members at Lake Forest High School is 15 years, and more than 85 percent of the faculty members hold the master's degree or beyond. Members of the faculty have been instrumental in the development of Advanced Placement courses, and many have pursued graduate study under grants from the National Science Foundation.

Figure 1

A profile of an outstanding public high school in Illinois gives prospective parents three pages of detailed information about the community, school facilities, faculty and student body. The profiles of average schools are often limited to one or two pages, while substandard schools do

The Curriculum

The academic offerings of Lake Forest High School are diverse and include traditional academic areas, fine arts and industrial technology. Greek and Latin remain part of the curriculum. Fifth-year foreign language study is offered as is an extensive list of Advanced Placement coursework.

The elective curriculum has grown to include vocational and work-related programs, special education and learning disabilities programs and computer-assisted instruction.

Graduation Requirements

Sixteen units of credit, divided as follow:

English	3 units
Mathematics	2 units

The second year requirement may be met by Electricity, Electronics or Engineering Drafting 1.

Science	1 unit
Social Studies	2 units

Must include 1 unit of United States history

Physical Education	1 unit

(1/8 unit per semester)

Electives	1 unit

May be completed through study of art, foreign language, music, business education, home arts, technology, telecommunications, C.O.E. or LCAVC.

Designation of Courses

Advanced Placement

College level courses which adhere to nationally standardized syllabi as proposed by the College Entrance Examination Board. AP courses represent the highest level of performance within a specified area.

Honors

Courses which provide enriched and/or accelerated curriculum requiring students to possess analytical thinking skills.

College Preparatory

Courses which require a mastery of fundamental skills allowing concentration on acquisition and application of new knowledge.

Concepts

Courses which provide review and remediation of basic skills that are essential to functioning in society.

Marking System

A⁺ A special grade indicating unusually brilliant achievement

A An honor grade indicating high achievement

B An honor grade for achievement considered above normal in terms of the course objectives

C The grade for achievement considered normal in reference to course objectives

D A special grade for students who are unable to accomplish minimum objectives of the course but who are making a noticeable effort to improve themselves in the skills and content of the subject

F Failure to accomplish minimum objectives of a course

WF Withdrawal from a course with failure

I Incomplete

P Pass, an option in one course for seniors only

E Medically excused

S Satisfactory

AU Audit

Distribution of Grades in Five Major Academic Areas

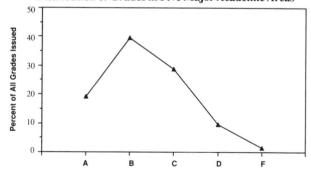

not even publish profiles for the public. For a quick, preliminary evaluation of a school, use Report Card No. 2 to compare data from school profiles with national averages. (A sample evaluation of this profile appears in Figure 2 in Chapter 6.)

Profile – Class of 1989

Distribution of Graduates

The members of the Class of 1989 made 1638 applications to 352 postsecondary institutions. Final plans of those students are as follow:

Number of Graduates	328
Enrolled in 4-year colleges	86%
Enrolled in 2-year colleges	6%
Employed	7%
Other	1%

Geographic Distribution of 4-year college matriculants

17 Illinois colleges	63 students
49 Midwestern colleges outside Illinois	107 students
28 Northeastern colleges	37 students
17 Southern Colleges	21 students
10 Southwestern and Mountain States colleges	27 students
9 Pacific Coast colleges	9 students
To foreign countries	6 students
Choices unknown	8 students

Merit Scholarship Data

National Merit Semi-finalists	2
National Merit Commended	16
Illinois State Scholars	76

Illinois Board of Higher Education Requirements

The table below shows the percentage of Lake Forest High School students who meet the requirements which have been established by the Illinois Board of Higher Education.

4 years of English	97%
3 years of mathematics	78%
3 years of social studies	67%
3 years of science	71%
2 years of foreign language	82%

SAT Data

SAT scores were reported by 88% of the graduates

Mean Scores

	LFHS	National
Verbal	469	427
Math	512	476

Mean Score Distribution by Rank in Class

	Verbal	Math
Top Decile	571	654
2nd Decile	538	592
2nd Quintile	463	517
3rd Quintile	433	463
4th Quintile	373	417
5th Quintile	408	340

ACT Data

ACT scores were reported by 84% of the graduates

Mean Scores

	LFHS	National
English	21.1	18.4
Math	21.9	17.1
Social Studies	21.4	17.2
Natural Science	24.5	21.2
Composite	22.4	18.6

Advanced Placement Data

Forty-nine students took 161 Advanced Placement exams in 16 areas. Scores of three or above were achieved by 82% of test takers.

Distribution of Advanced Placement

American History	17 students
Biology	8 students
Chemistry	10 students
Computer Science	1 student
Economics – Micro	14 students
Economics – Macro	13 students
English Language and Composition	1 student
English Literature and Composition	22 students
European History	18 students
French Language	8 students
German Language	2 students
Government and Politics American	15 students
Government and Politics Comparative	15 students
Math Calculus BC	11 students
Physics B	3 students
Spanish Language	3 students
TOTAL AP Exams	**161**

unnecessary trips to substandard schools. (Figure 2 in Chapter 6 is a sample evaluation.) If profiles are not available at the school superintendent's office, try to get them at school administration offices. (Most available public high school profiles are published annually in the *College Board Guide to High Schools*, available in many public libraries or from the College Board in New York [1-800-323-7155] for $89.50.)

Again, school districts with substandard education may refuse to provide profiles or say they don't compile them. Only about 40% of American high schools and less than 10% of elementary schools publish profiles. And data in profiles is public information, of course, but heavyhanded demands for them will only lead to angry confrontation and, in the end, accomplish little. If the superintendent's office refuses to give you the information you want, simply accept the experience as an indication of a poor school system and spend your energies looking for a better one elsewhere—regardless of how attracted you may be to an area or a house you saw for sale.

The School Board

Assuming you receive a friendly reception and obtain all the data you need about local schools, be sure to get the following additional information:

1. *The names of the superintendent of schools and all school board members;* also, their backgrounds, education, professional preparation for service on the school board and views about education and why they ran for election or were appointed. The superintendent's office should have a resume for each member and some documents outlining each member's views. Local newspapers should also have that information. It's important to know whether the community elected its school board to improve education or to ban books or to impose unconstitutional, anti-education measures such as prayer in school and "creation science."
2. *Agendas (not the minutes) of school board meetings for the last 12 months.* From these you'll be able to see the board's primary concerns. Are they concerned mostly with quality of education or quality of sports teams? Again, look for anti-education issues such as banning books or sex education, instituting prayer in school and imposing creation science. The primary concerns of school boards automatically echo through the corridors of schools they govern and, depending on the educational goals you have for your children, should influence your choice of school district.

The makeup of the school board and its agendas will also tell you who governs the district's schools—professional educators or politicians and special interest groups.

The Superintendent

In addition to the background of school board members, it's important to get information about the superintendent's background, education, professional training and views on education (see Report Card No. 3). Then, make an appointment for a personal interview to probe into the quality of the district's schools.

Accreditation

The first and most important question to ask the superintendent is whether schools in the district are accredited by the regional accreditation association. "Accreditation" is *not* the same as "certification"— and don't let anyone try to confuse you by using the terms interchangeably. Every state requires every school to be certified, which is nothing more than legal approval to operate. Depending on state laws, certification may only mean adherence to fire safety laws. States also require all teachers to be certified—they must meet certain minimum requirements to obtain a license to teach in each state—none of which has a thing to do with school accreditation.

Accreditation is a complex examination conducted every one to four years. The school's educational goals and standards are studied by respected educators from other schools in the region. (There are six regions in the United States.) The most selective colleges and universities invariably prefer applicants from accredited high schools.

Accreditation is voluntary and is granted only to schools that meet the minimum standards of each regional association. These standards may differ slightly for public, private and church-related schools, and the standards differ somewhat from region to region. All six accreditation associations demand that member schools have clearly stated educational goals and methods for achieving those goals. The goals may differ, according to the student community, but whatever the goals are, accreditation will depend on a school's success in achieving them.

In addition, some accreditation associations require all teachers to have at least a bachelor's degree from an *accredited* college or university and at least eight college courses in each subject they teach. Principals must have at least a master's degree—again, from an accredited university. Some accreditation association standards specify the minimum number of books and periodicals each library must have—no less than 4,000 books, no matter how small the school, and at least 10 books (not including textbooks) for every student. Some associations also list acceptable teacher-pupil ratios, minimum acceptable student achievement levels, the minimum number of subjects and courses the school must teach in each grade and the acceptable materials it must provide for those courses.

Association names, addresses and telephone numbers are listed after the Checklist at the end of this chapter. The associations are not connected with any government agencies, although some states (Connecticut, for example) refuse to certify a school that has not gained accreditation. The associations are privately operated and run by leading educators from member schools interested in improving the quality of education in their areas. They welcome all inquiries from parents.

Only about 40% of elementary schools across the United States and 60% of high schools are accredited. In some areas, as few as 10% of schools are accredited. There are many reasons that many schools either refuse to meet or cannot meet the minimum educational standards of the regional accreditation associations. In some instances, politicians at the state or local level interfere with accreditation to avoid losing control of schools to professional educators; in other instances, communities refuse to provide schools with enough money for the facilities required for accreditation. In some cases, teacher unions block accreditation to prevent discharge of incompetent teachers. So, by all means, check with the appropriate association to see if the school you are considering for your child is accredited or not. If not, find out why before condemning it as substandard. Occasionally, the school population is so small (as in many isolated rural areas) that the school cannot afford to provide all the facilities required for accreditation—a large library, for example, or extensive laboratory facilities for biology, chemistry and physics. In other words, there can be perfectly valid reasons for lack of accreditation that may not reflect on the quality of education—only on the quantity and variety.

Small schools can, however, compensate for lack of costly facilities by entering into cooperative arrangements with other small schools and with public libraries to share common facilities. Good small schools do just that. For average-sized schools in average income areas, however, there are usually no valid reasons for lack of accreditation. Every school in the United States has at its disposal a set of fine educational standards set by the six accreditation associations. A school that refuses to adopt those standards obviously does not care about educational excellence for its students.

As a rule, therefore, if you want the best possible education for your children, don't send them to unaccredited schools, whether they are public or private.

Curriculum Audits

In addition to accreditation, many outstanding schools willingly submit to a "curriculum audit" by the American Association of School Administrators. Under an AASA audit, a team of auditors spends a week examining every aspect of a school's curriculum and teaching methods to see if they meet national standards. An audit exposes all the faults of a school's faculty and curriculum—as well as its strengths.

Obviously, it takes courage and confidence in one's school and faculty to submit to such an audit, and few substandard schools dare do so. Be sure to ask the superintendent whether the schools in the district have done so. If not, why not?

Decision Making

Another important area to probe during your interview with the superintendent is who governs the district's schools (see Report Card No. 4). As mentioned earlier, districts with the best schools hire the best professional educators they can find and give them complete autonomy to run schools free of interference from nonprofessionals. Some key questions to ask in this area include:

- Who makes the major educational decisions in each of the district's schools—the principals and teachers or school board members and state educational authorities?
- Do teachers design their own courses and select textbooks, or are lesson plans and reading materials imposed by higher authorities? As mentioned earlier, 21 state governments (mostly in the South and Southwest), dictate the choice of textbooks for all teachers in all grades in those states. Some even impose lesson plans on teachers. The teachers in those states are among the lowest paid in the United States, and quality of education is equally low.
- Who sets standards of student behavior and determines student promotions and retentions? (Find out, too, what teachers report as their major problems with students at school. That's a major factor in determining school district quality. Nationally, 54% report drugs a problem, according to the U.S. Department of Education; 49% say alcohol is a problem; 36% report racial discord; 44% list violence between students; and 24% list violence against teachers.)
- Who has authority over school budget allocations and spending—school principals, the superintendent or the school board?
- Who has authority over teacher hiring and firing and teacher evaluation—the superintendent and school board or the principal and faculty peer-review committees?

All these questions, of course, are designed to determine who runs schools in the district—professional educators or noneducators. Keep in mind that education at the finest private schools and universities in the United States is controlled by professional educators. Their boards of directors concern themselves primarily with fund-raising and broad policy decisions to improve academic standings of the schools they govern. Top-ranked public school districts operate the same way, according to a U.S. Department of Education study of America's most successful public schools. In the districts of those schools, school boards concern themselves only with getting the necessary funding for budgets proposed by the professional educators who run the schools. They do not involve themselves with curriculum planning or textbook choices or teacher evaluation. They try to recruit and hire the finest professional educators they can find and afford and then leave educating to the "pros."

INTERVIEWS WITH SCHOOL AND COMMUNITY BOARD MEMBERS

In addition to interviewing the superintendent of schools, it can help to interview one or more members of the school board—especially in small communities where such personal contacts are relatively easy to make. Again, the reception you get will add more pluses or minuses to your evaluation of the school district. Ask board members the same questions you asked the superintendent. See if their answers agree. Fill in Report Card No. 3 with the details of each board member's personal background that you may not have been able to get at the superintendent's office—especially views on education, goals, stands on anti-education issues and reasons for serving on the board. Find out about their experience in education and how their education, jobs and background qualify them to sit on a school board.

Besides the superintendent and the school board, you'll undoubtedly get appraisals of local schools from other members of the community, such as parents and merchants. By all means ask them whether they think the schools are good and what they consider the best qualities of each school. Ask also whether they feel they have adequate access to the principal and faculty. But remember that they are not professional educators, and it is not wise to put too much stock in their opinions about educational methods. Above all, under no circumstances should you turn to or listen to real estate agents for such an appraisal. In the first place, they seldom have any professional knowledge about schools. Secondly, they want you to buy or rent, and it's almost always in their interests to tell you, "The schools here are wonderful."

So rely on your own observations and the results you get from the Report Cards in Part II to evaluate a district and its schools. If the F's for Inferior outnumber the A's for Above Average on the first four Report Cards (school district, school profile, school board and professional input), you can skip any further investigation of the schools in the area and look elsewhere. If the A's outnumber the F's, on the other hand, it will certainly be worthwhile making an in-depth evaluation of individual schools in the district. The chapters that follow will show you how.

If school district A's and F's balance each other out and district schools only appear average or "satisfactory" ("S"), see if you can't find a better district elsewhere. If you can't, you can always come back and evaluate individual schools later on.

ALTERNATIVES

If educational quality is low in the state in which you are looking, check the possibility of living in an adjacent or nearby state with better education and commuting to work in the state with the poorer system. That's especially easy in bistate and tristate areas. In the New York metropolitan area, for example, you could live or work in New York, New Jersey or Connecticut and commute to and from any of the three states.

If living out of state is geographically impossible, try to find at least a few or even one public school district in the state that is above average for the state and the United States.

Many states allow you to live in one district and send your children to school in other districts if you pay full costs of tuition. Some states are also experimenting with "voucher" systems that transfer the tax monies that would have been spent on education in a child's home district to the district where he or she actually attends school.

Some states and cities also have magnet schools, highly selective public schools designed for gifted students and to which any student in the state or area may apply. Some specialize in the arts or sciences; others offer broad curricula. Check with the state superintendent of schools or the board of education in each district to see if the city, county or state has such magnet schools.

If all districts in the area prove equally poor and there are no magnet schools, start looking at nearby private and church-related schools. It's essential, though, that any private or church-related school you consider be accredited. Unlike school boards, the boards of directors or trustees of private and church-related schools do not have to answer to the general public. That can be good or bad. On the one hand, they can pursue the highest educational goals for their children and adopt innovative teaching methods without interference by politically motivated bureaucrats. For more than a century, the top-ranked independent, private day schools and boarding schools (mostly in the Northeast) have provided the finest primary and secondary school education in the United States and, in many cases, the world. Their students usually rank among the academic elite of the U.S. student population—on college admissions tests, admission to the most selective colleges, academic performance at college and achievement later in life.

On the other hand, there are many substandard private schools. The same independence that allows one board of trustees to pursue the highest educational goals, free of government interference, allows another board to pursue substandard goals that interfere with good education. In many areas of the South, for example, parents' groups have established all-white private schools and academies to perpetuate racial segregation. Because of extremely poor educational quality, many have been unable to earn accreditation by the Southern Association of Colleges and Schools. So just because a school is private and independent does not necessarily make it good.

You can find all you need about virtually every U.S. private school in *Peterson's Guide to Independent Secondary Schools*. A large proportion of them operate or work with "feeder" elementary schools as well, so you can use the *Guide* to find good schools for preschoolers as well as older children. The *Guide* has done all the research into the quality of the schools listed. You'll have nothing to do but call the schools near you and make an appointment to meet the principal and teachers and tour the facilities. Good private schools encourage parents to visit, and they invite prospective students to spend a day or more attending classes and participating in school activities. And don't let the term "private school" scare you away—regardless of costs. All private schools offer scholarships, educational loans and other financial aid, just as all colleges and universities do. Indeed, 20% to 40% of students at the top-ranked private day schools and boarding schools in the United States receive financial aid. *Peterson's Guide* lists the percentage for each school.

If there are no acceptable private schools in or near your area, another educational option—for adolescents only—is boarding school. Again, *Peterson's Guide* is the best reference.

For children too young for boarding school, another course of action, if there are no good private schools nearby, is to enroll them in local public schools and supplement their education with tutoring—either by hiring a private tutor or doing the job yourself. During the early years of schooling, such extra tutoring is not only enormously beneficial, it is also great fun for many children if presented in the right way. But don't expect your children to obtain a good education this way in a substandard school system with unqualified faculties and low academic standards. First of all, the education isn't there to obtain. Secondly, pressures from peers who hold academic achievement in low esteem will eventually influence your children and make it difficult or impossible to achieve academically. In such schools, "brains" are ridiculed as "nerds," and academic achievers are not only ostracized socially, they are often attacked physically. If you expect your children to be academic achievers, you will certainly risk making them extremely unhappy by sending them to substandard schools.

As for average schools, a good education is usually there for the taking by academically aggressive youngsters who are strong enough to withstand peer pressures for academic mediocrity. Again, though, academic achievers often face social ostracism and occasional physical abuse by the nonachievers who usually make up the majority of student bodies in average schools. You'll have to monitor the situation carefully. It's far preferable for academic achievers to attend superior schools with other students like themselves who hold knowledge in high esteem. That's why, if you find your family trapped in an area with substandard or mediocre public schools, I strongly advise sending your children to an independent or private day school. If there is none nearby, carefully investigate private boarding schools if you value your children's educational futures.

CHECKLIST

Evaluating State and District School Systems

☐ State system (compare with national averages). (See Figs. 1 and 2.)

☐ School district

— Compare with national and state averages (Report Card No. 1).

— Check accreditation of local schools. If not accredited, why not? (See below for list of accreditation commissions.)

— Obtain school profiles. Compare with national averages for quick, preliminary evaluations (Report Card No. 2).

— Check credentials of superintendent and school board members.

— Curriculum audit.

— Determine who runs the schools by conducting interviews with superintendent and school board members.

— Identify major teacher problems with students.

— Investigate alternative schools.

— Magnet schools.

— Other school districts.

— Private day schools (see *Peterson's Guide to Independent Secondary Schools*).

— Private boarding schools (see *Peterson's*).

THE SIX REGIONAL SCHOOL ACCREDITATION COMMISSIONS

New England Association of Schools and Colleges (Maine, New Hampshire, Vermont, Massachusetts, Rhode Island, Connecticut), The Sanborn House, 15 High St., Winchester, MA 01890. Tel: (617) 729–6762.

Middle States Association of Colleges and Schools (New York, New Jersey, Pennsylvania, Delaware, Maryland, District of Columbia), 3624 Market St., Philadelphia, PA 19104. Tel: (215) 662–5600.

Southern Association of Colleges and Schools (Kentucky, Virginia, Tennessee, North Carolina, South Carolina, Georgia, Florida, Alabama, Mississippi, Louisiana, Texas), 1866 Southern Lane, Decatur, GA 30033. Tel: (404) 329-6500.

North Central Association of Colleges and Schools (North Dakota, South Dakota, Minnesota, Wisconsin, Michigan, Ohio, West Virginia, Indiana, Illinois, Iowa, Nebraska, Wyoming, Colorado, Kansas, Missouri, Arkansas, Oklahoma, New Mexico, Arizona), 1540 30th St., Boulder, CO 80306. Tel: (800) 525–9517.

Northwest Association of Schools and Colleges (Alaska, Washington, Oregon, Idaho, Montana, Nevada, Utah), Education Building No. 528, Boise State University, Boise, ID 83725. Tel: (208) 385-1596.

Western Association of Schools and Colleges (California, Hawaii, Guam, American Samoa), 1606 Rollins Road, Burlingame, CA 94010. Tel: (415) 697-7711.

CHAPTER 3

SCHOOL QUALITY: A QUICK APPRAISAL

By now you should have a pretty good idea of the quality of education in the states and school districts where your children may attend school. It's now time to look at individual schools, and that will mean one or more visits to each school where your children might enroll.

Remember, once again, it may be unfair to "want it all"—to expect to find the "perfect" school for your children and to expect the school you choose to remain perfect in every category of instruction every year your children attend. There are bound to be disappointments along the way—a grouchy teacher your child is convinced "hates me" or an incompetent teacher or a useless required course. In general, though, you have a right to expect your children's schools to adhere to acceptable educational standards, and you should not consider sending your children to any school that cannot or will not do so.

Again, the standards outlined below are the *minimum acceptable standards* of the six regional accreditation commissions and also of private and government study groups and the U.S. Department of Education. So, what you'll be asking of each school—public, private or church-related—is simply a sound education for your children. Accept nothing less!

PHYSICAL CONDITION

The first step in evaluating a school is a preliminary visit to gain a general impression of the school's physical and social environment. Record your impressions from this preliminary visit on Report Card No. 8. Look around the neighborhood. Does it seem clean, orderly, safe? Walk or drive a short way in each direction. Your children may have to! Take a long look. Don't hurry. If you're in doubt about neighborhood safety, visit or call the local police department and speak to the community affairs officer. This can be particularly helpful in large cities where you're unfamiliar with different neighborhoods.

Take a long look, too, at the school yard and the building exterior. Are they attractive, safe and well maintained? Is the fencing in good shape? Does the building seem well cared for, or is it covered with patches and repairs? Are there broken windows? Is there any graffiti? Are kids or adults loitering outside the school property? What kind of equipment is in the school yard? In elementary schools, there should be ample playground equipment—even in the middle of big cities. Suburban and rural middle schools and high schools should have playing fields with such equipment as batting cages and goal posts—and perhaps tennis courts. (The sports facilities of urban high schools are often in other parts of the city, separate from school buildings.) If you're looking at an elementary school, see if the equipment is in good repair. Is there enough of it for the number of youngsters it must serve?

A community and school administration that does not care enough to provide and maintain its school building and equipment properly probably does not care enough to give its children a good education. Enter your findings by putting a check under "A" for above average, "S" for satisfactory or "F" for inferior opposite each facility listed on Report Card No. 8, School Facilities.

SCHOOL INTERIOR

As you enter the school, once again look at the physical condition—the floors, walls and ceilings. Are they well maintained and attractive? Do hallways have a happy look, with children's art work on the walls—or are they scarred and dismal-looking and decorated only with graffiti or mimeographed notices from the school bureaucracy? Are hallways well-lit? Are floors clean or littered? Remember, this is the atmosphere in which your children will face the educational process. Make certain it's a pleasant place that will feed their enthusiasm.

Keep a sharp eye out for safety provisions—fire extinguishers and well-marked fire exits. As many as one-quarter of the schools in some areas fail to meet fire and safety regulations.

Does the place smell clean? Is it hot and stuffy or cold and damp? More than one-quarter of all U.S. schools have outdated or nonfunctioning heating and air-conditioning equipment. Look for ramps and other facilities for handicapped children, staff and faculty members. More than 10% of U.S. schools disobey federal laws requiring such facilities. Again, it's a reflection of the degree of caring by the community and school administration. A school that does not meet the individual needs of its handicapped children seldom meets the individual needs of any of its children.

In addition to the physical look of the school, pay attention to the social look. What is the noise level in the corridors during and between classes? Are students milling about, leaning against corridor walls or sitting on hallway floors during classtime, with no apparent academic obligations to keep them busy? Do they wear Walkmans? Is there shouting or shoving or fighting? Does noise emanate from classrooms? Look in if you can. Do they appear overcrowded, with kids leaning against walls or seated on window sills or on the floor? Is the atmosphere filled with the constant ringing of bells and blasts of loudspeaker announcements?

What, in other words, is the atmosphere of the school? Are you walking through halls of learning or a "blackboard jungle"? Look into children's faces? Are they happy, pensive, fearful, angry? Talk to them. Ask for directions to the principal's office. How do they respond? Do they think it's a good school? Why? What don't they like about it?

THE ADMINISTRATION OFFICE

As you enter the administration office, see if it is filled with students. That's usually a sign of problems. Schools with quality education do not burden students with administrative red tape or require their constant presence in the office instead of the classroom, where they belong.

Note, especially, the attitude of staff members—to students, on the one hand, and to you as you enter. Are staffers warm toward the children? Do they respond quickly to your presence—and in a friendly manner? Or do they act cold and unforgiving toward kids and ignore you while they shuffle papers and fill out forms.

A school that does a good job educating its children cares about their feelings and the feelings of the adults in the community that support the school.

SCHOOL CATALOGS

Ask for all available printed materials—a school profile (see Figure 1 in Chapter 2), a course catalog, a set of school rules and regulations and a descriptive booklet about the school and its parents' organizations. Although some school booklets are quite lavishly illustrated, others may simply be a set of mimeographed pages stapled together. The format is unimportant. What is important is that the school have documents describing its academic programs, academic goals, special programs, guidance services, faculty and their backgrounds, meal services, cultural programs, extracurricular activities, student organizations and athletics. All good public and private schools have such printed materials, and they'll gladly mail them to you if you live too far away or it's inconvenient for you to pick them up. The materials will give you much of the data you'll need for the Report Cards for school evaluations in Part II.

As in the district superintendent's office, warm smiles from the staff in the school administration office will tell you a great deal about the school. A friendly "May I help you?" and a willingness to share facts, figures, triumphs and failures are evidence of a strong school that does not fear comparison with other schools. Indeed, after heaping more materials in your arms than you expect, staffers at a superior school will probably ask you to wait so the principal or assistant principal can be told of your presence and greet you personally. You'll know immediately that a school is below average if staffers and their superiors refuse to provide the information you want or say they have no such materials. That's a signal they don't want to publicize how poor their school is. Such schools may also refuse to let you tour the building or visit classes.

As in the superintendent's office, angry demands will accomplish nothing and will certainly not transform a substandard school into a superior one in time to affect your children's education. It is far more productive to direct your attention and your children elsewhere.

A superior school will, however, invite you to meet adminstrators, tour the school, sit in on classes and meet teachers and parents. And by all means, make appointments to do so. If time and distance are not a factor, it's best if you make such an in-depth visit on another day—to give you time to absorb what you've seen on your first visit and to study the school's printed materials. There's only so much anyone can absorb in one visit—whether it's to a museum or a school. Staying too long is usually nonproductive. You'll gain far more insight into the school after you've had time to fill in some of the Report Cards in Part II and develop a list of searching questions unanswered by school catalogs and brochures. The rest of this chapter discusses what to look for in those booklets.

Goals

Clearly stated educational goals are a key difference between a school offering quality education and one that is a mere caretaker. The six regional accreditation associations require member schools to put their goals or "philosophy" in writing, and you should be able to find them in either the descriptive booklet about the school or at the beginning of the course catalog. All good schools have such goals.

"To prepare students for higher education and responsible citizenship" is the clearly stated goal of a private college preparatory school in Connecticut. A high school in a wealthy Chicago suburb states that most (but not all) of its curriculum "is college preparatory." A Vermont public high school, with a big vocational as well as academic program, lists among its primary goals the teaching of "skills in reading, writing, mathematics and reasoning" and skills for "a satisfying and worthwhile life." All three schools are good ones, but each obviously has different goals that reflect the needs of its student constituency and affect its educational atmosphere.

Schools at all grade levels should have clearly stated goals. An outstanding New York primary school, for example, says its goal is "to contribute to a child's development by providing sensitive, intelligent teachers who respond to . . . each child's special pattern of growth, physically, emotionally, socially and intellectually." The school goes on to describe its "setting, where children can proceed at an individual pace (and) fulfill their potential for development . . ." Here the emphasis is on the individuality of each child rather than on lockstep learning.

A few years ago, then–Secretary of Education William J. Bennett wrote what he felt should be the educational goals of all U.S. elementary and middle schools:

> We want our students—by the end of 8th grade—to read, write and speak clear grammatical English and to be acquainted with the varieties and qualities of fiction and nonfiction literature. We want them to know the essential features of American and world history, the major landscapes and nations of the earth, and the rights and obligations that belong to citizens of the United States. We want them to be proficient in arithmetic and geometry, and familiar with basic principles of algebra. We want them to have begun exploring biology, chemistry, physics, and a foreign language; to have investigated the history and practice of art and music; and to have developed the habits of health, fitness, and athletic fair play. In short, we want our elementary school graduates to be fully prepared for serious and challenging study in high school.

In fairness to your children, you should not enroll them in an elementary school that does not subscribe to these goals as *minimum* standards.

Clearly stated educational goals are important for three reasons. First, they give the faculty and staff a clear policy for working with students (and you should check that the principal and teachers can actually cite the school's goals when you interview them). Second, they tell students what is expected of them. And lastly, they give parents a chance to compare the school's goals with their own and, if the differences are too great, to enroll their children elsewhere. Clear goals tell you unequivocally the emphasis placed on academics, individual creativity, ethical conduct, athletics, extracurricular activities and community service—and whether there is too much emphasis on one at the expense of another.

Rules and Regulations

The descriptive booklet or catalog should also list school rules and regulations. Obviously, the rules and regulations for elementary schools, especially kindergartners, will be quite different from those for middle schools and high schools. For younger children, the goal of a good elementary school is to encourage good work habits by establishing order with firm but fair discipline. A good school should be able to impose discipline flexibly, on a case-by-case basis, in cooperation with parents—rather than in a heavy-handed bureacratic way that ignores individual circumstances.

Flexibility, however, should not deteriorate into indecision—especially in middle schools and high schools, where adolescents desperately need firm guidance. All the best middle schools and high schools have clearly defined, strictly enforced rules of academic conduct and social behavior. At those levels, school catalogs should clearly indicate school policies for handling misconduct, absenteeism, lateness, disruptive behavior, cheating, vandalism, violence, physical threats or verbal abuse, theft, weapons, racism or bigotry, gambling, use of tobacco, drugs or alcohol and even use of radios and tape players with headphones. The rules should state whether there is a dress code and a code of conduct for students when they are not in school. Social chaos usually results in schools without clearly stated and firmly enforced rules and regulations—and well-defined penalties for violations. Good schools usually handle first offenses for most infractions with a warning that parents will be notified of any second offense and perhaps called to school for a conference. A third offense usually leads to loss of school privileges or even suspension, depending on the severity of the offense, and a fourth infraction can lead to expulsion. Offenses that are serious felonies in the adult world—possession or sale of drugs, for example— should lead to expulsion after the first or second offense.

In any case, school catalogs should clearly state the rules and the punishments for violating rules. Remember, the less social discipline a school imposes on students, the less academic discipline it can impose and the more your children will have to rely on you and their own consciences for discipline. It's a lot to demand of children—especially young ones—to show self-discipline and restraint while their peers act chaotically. Look for another school if the booklet does not detail its rules of social conduct or if the rules seem lax.

Another thing to determine (so you're not shocked later on) is whether the school allows corporal punishment. Only 11 states forbid corporal punishment in school—Maine, Vermont, New Hampshire, Massachusetts, Rhode Island, New York, New Jersey, Maryland, Ohio, California and Hawaii.

In the section on rules, look also to see where authority rests in the school. Educators agree that decisions regarding a youngster should be made by those who know that youngster best and can tailor decisions to individual needs. The people who know students best in any school are their teachers. Schools with the highest quality of education give teachers decision-making authority over student discipline as well as academics. Youngsters simply do not respect and will not learn much from teachers with no authority. Although the principal in each school should be the ultimate authority, teacher authority over student behavior and student retention and promotion is usually another sign of a well-run school with high quality education. Unfortunately, fewer than half the teachers in U.S. schools now have such authority.

School Organization

The school booklets should tell you the size of the school, which is seldom a problem for stand-alone elementary schools. Two-thirds of the 59,000 elementary schools in the United States have fewer than 500 students. Because small children need so much individual attention, it's not a good idea to enroll them in schools larger than that unless the children are assured of being in small, carefully supervised groups both in and out of class.

The problem of size becomes far more difficult to avoid for students in seventh through twelfth grades. They usually have to attend huge central district schools. Of the nearly 27,000 secondary schools in the United States, nearly one-quarter have enrollments of 1,000 or more students, and more than 10% have enrollments of 1,500 to 3,000 or more students—far too large for effective learning, unless they are organized into "houses," or small "schools within a school."

Budget restrictions have made school size an enormous problem in many areas. It can be an important factor in educational quality and the ability of your children to achieve. It's frightening for most children to make the transition from elementary school to middle school and high school. Elementary schools are usually neighborhood schools that provide warmth and intimacy among neighborhood friends. Students grow to trust and often love their elementary school teachers, who usually teach the same group of students every day for an entire year and sometimes two. Most learning takes place in one classroom, which itself becomes a stable home away from home, where children can see their art displayed and feel free to leave treasured personal possessions.

Then, just as they reach early adolescence and need even more security, they are thrust into large, often impersonal, secondary schools, where mobs of older students brush past, presenting few friendly faces. Often these older students bully younger students. Throughout the day, harsh bells shock students out of their seats and send them scurrying down long corridors from classroom to classroom, each with a different teacher and a different, distant face. None is likely to be familiar with, let alone know, the special needs of each student.

Studies show that students in small schools perform better and participate in more activities than they do in large schools—especially shy or marginal students. Most young adolescents need the emotional security of belonging to a small community of students and adults who care about each other, know each other intimately and work together to achieve common goals.

Large schools are usually divisive in their effects on students. Socially aggressive "achievers" invariably dominate most activities—academics, sports and extracurricular activities; a much larger "middle" group of more passive students participates in relatively few or no activities; and a third group of nonachievers, "outsiders," as they're often called, usually takes part in no activities, does poorly in academics and is often responsible for disruptive behavior in or near school.

It is more difficult for students to develop a sense of being an "outsider" in the intimacy of small schools. The result is a much greater sense of community and far lower and often nonexistent crime or disruptive behavior.

So, if you have a choice, try to send your children to smaller schools. That should not be too difficult. Almost half (46%) the 27,000 secondary schools in the United States have fewer than 500 students, and anther 30 percent have between 500 and 1,000. These smaller schools should be able to offer the warmth and security needed for youngsters to excel if the academic quality is high enough.

One disadvantage of small schools is that they often cannot afford the vast facilities of large schools nor can they usually offer as wide a variety of courses. But top-quality small schools compensate for lack of on-campus facilities by sharing facilities with other schools or by taking advantage of off-campus facilities such as town or county libraries, museums, concert halls, theaters, wildlife refuges, national or state parks, colleges or universities, local industries and all the other off-campus institutions that can complement school education. High-quality schools also try to recruit parttime professionals as volunteers to teach students. The school's booklet should describe these efforts.

As for the nearly 25% of U.S. secondary schools that have more than 1,000 students, some do offer warmth and security to their students, along with high quality education. They often do so by organizing themselves into smaller units—"schools within a school," or "houses." The booklets from each school will certainly describe such systems of organization if they have them.

Each "house" should indeed be a small school, consisting, ideally, of about 100 students (no more than 200) and five to 10 teachers. The teachers work as a team to teach a core curriculum of English, math, science, foreign language, history and the arts, usually along a separate corridor with its own classrooms and administrative office. No class has more than 15 to 20 students, and students in each house and their teachers remain together for a minimum of two years. Each teacher has a homeroom, and each serves as a confidential advisor/advocate for individual students. The members of each house—students and teachers—can call upon the umbrella "super-school" for facilities that no individual house could afford on its own. Thus, all houses share athletic facilities. Most students in each house participate in intramural athletics and play teams from other houses, but individual athletes may try out for varsity teams that represent the entire school in interscholastic sports. Similarly, all houses share science laboratories or art and music facilities, although each house has exclusive use of the facilities in its time slot and never uses them at the same time as other houses.

Such houses also avoid "tracking" as much as possible. Tracking is a method of teaching by which students are grouped according to ability. Homogeneous grouping, as tracking is called in education, often begins in first grade and, at that age, it usually reflects a child's rate of development rather than innate abilities. Many "slow" first graders turn out to be gifted fourth graders—and vice versa—if they stay in mixed groups of normal children with different abilities and talents.

Unfortunately, tracking is often a self-fulfilling prophecy that can be devastating for children in kindergarten and the early grades. Grouped together, slow students are condemned to a form of environmental retardation. They are often assigned to the least qualified teachers who treat them as incompetents and seldom ask them to excel. They usually remain slow students throughout their school years because children tend to perform according to the expectations of adults around them. As they reach early adolescence, many become behavior problems in response to their academic failures. Ultimately, tracking can lead to an adult life of failure, unemployment and poverty. It is a teaching practice that parents who are seeking the best for their children should avoid.

Top-ranked schools at all levels—elementary, middle and high school—have found that heterogeneous grouping usually helps all students excel, including the academically gifted, who, in high school, often tutor slower, average students, with startling improvements for both. Among the 200 elementary and middle public schools cited by the Department of Education as the best in the United States, fewer than 30% still grouped students in tracks based on academic achievement.

Better quality high schools are also abandoning curricular tracking that leads to academic, general and vocational diplomas. Indeed, top quality schools have abandoned the directionless "general track" that produces two-thirds of all high school dropouts in the United States. Instead, they group students heterogeneously in all but specialized courses. All students study a single core curriculum that fulfills the requirements of both college and the marketplace and gives every student the option of going to college or to work after graduation. All receive the same high school diploma. During their last two years of high school, some de facto curricular tracking occurs as those who are certain they want to go to college supplement the core curriculum with advanced academic electives. Those interested in going into business or industry take electives in those fields. In neither case do students eliminate any options. The doors to college remain open to all.

So, if you're looking at high schools, be certain they require all students, regardless of postsecondary school plans, to take a core curriculum, choosing courses all from the academics track only, preferably from the honors program (see Part III). The National Commission on Excellence in Education a decade ago said that no American student should graduate from high school without completing at least four years of English and three years each of social studies, mathematics, science and a foreign language, all from the academic or honors tracks. Under no circumstances should you permit your children to take any courses from the general studies program, which no selective colleges will accept in fulfillment of high school course requirements. General studies are considered so poor that some states are outlawing them. Two U.S. presidents and the governors of all 50 states agree. All top quality high schools now realize that all students need—and indeed, have a right to—a basic core of knowledge that is essential to all Americans to function effectively as adults in a free, self-governing society.

Former Secretary of Education William J. Bennett put it this way:

> We want our students—whatever their plans for the future—to take from high school a shared body of knowledge and skills, a common language of ideas, a common moral and intellectual discipline. We want them to know math and science, history and literature. We want them to know how to think for themselves, to respond to important questions, to solve problems, to pursue an argument, to defend a point of view, to understand its opposite, and to weigh alternatives. We want them to develop,

through example and experience, those habits of mind and traits of character properly prized by society. And we want them to be prepared for entry into the community of responsible adults.

As a parent, consumer and taxpayer, you have the right to expect no less for your children from any public high school in America!

Senior Class Profile

High school booklets should also include a profile (see Figure 1 in Chapter 2) of its most recent graduating class. If you didn't receive this at the superintendent's office, ask for it from the school administration. It's important to know the school's graduation and dropout rates and the percentage of seniors who go to college and to compare their Scholastic Aptitude Test scores and other college entrance examination scores with the requirements of selective colleges and national averages. Although not all students take SATs, the average score of those who do usually reflect the academic quality of the entire school. These comparisons can give you a quick appraisal of the school's academic standards (see Figure 2 in Chapter 6 and Report Card No. 2). Don't put too much stock in so-called "tests" that measure whether students in lower grades are performing above, below or at grade levels, unless they are tests that are prepared and administered by independent testing agencies that radically change the test questions every year. Unfortunately, most such achievement tests are usually administered by teachers in school instead of independent administrators. State aid is often tied to test scores, and many schools order teachers to ignore essential course material and concentrate on preparing students to score well on tests. Because questions remain essentially the same from year to year, that's easy to do, and high scores are often the rule in even the worst schools.

Descriptive booklets should also tell you something about the faculty and administrators and their educational backgrounds. Lake Forest High School in Illinois says that "85 percent of faculty members hold the master's degree or beyond" and that the average faculty member has worked at the school for 15 years—a sure sign of faculty contentment that undoubtedly contributes to the high percentage (86%) of the school's seniors who go on to four-year colleges. School booklets should list all recreational, athletic and extracurricular activities available to students, although you'll learn much more about these, as well as the faculty, if and when you decide to tour the school.

Administrative Services

School booklets should describe all administrative services and plant facilities, such as health care (is there a fulltime registered nurse?), transportation (does the district provide bus service for school at normal hours *and* for after-school activities?) and after-school child-care programs for working parents and for emergencies. Does the school offer special education for handicapped children and tutoring programs for children who may be behind in certain areas? Ask also about homebound instruction for children who may be bedridden for an extended period. And don't forget to ask about psychological services. Counseling may not be essential for educational quality, but it certainly is a plus for many children. In this area, too, find out how the school handles disruptive high-risk students in trouble with drugs, alcohol, mental illness or emotional problems.

At high schools, find out what kind of guidance services the school provides. Does each student have a faculty advisor as well as a guidance counselor? The average guidance counselor in U.S. high schools is responsible for more than 400 students, with a result that too few students receive adequate counseling. Even 50 students are too many for a single counselor—which is why top-quality high schools provide each student with a faculty advisor as an adult friend/advocate who can complement the guidance counselor. In addition, top schools have at least two teams of guidance specialists—one for college admissions counseling of college-bound students, the other for career counseling of students interested in jobs in industrial trades and business. (Some high schools also offer elective courses on job placement skills, occupational exploration and "The World of Work" as part of their guidance programs.)

CHECKLIST
Evaluating Schools

☐ Preliminary visit to the school
  ___ Neighborhood quality
  ___ School grounds and building
  ___ School interior
    ___ Physical condition
    ___ Atmosphere
☐ Administration office
  ___ Atmosphere
  ___ Availability of printed materials
  ___ Appointments to tour school, visit classes, meet teachers and principal
☐ School catalogs and brochures
  ___ Description of school and goals
  ___ Rules and regulations

_____ School size and organization
   _____ "Schools within a school" or "houses"
   _____ Tracking (By ability? By curriculum [academic, general, vocational]?)
_____ Course catalog (compare with Part III, "The Academic Curriculum")
   _____ Core curriculum
   _____ Graduation requirements
_____ Senior class profile (for high schools)
_____ Faculty and administration profile
_____ Sports and extracurricular activities
_____ Administrative services
   _____ Health office
   _____ Transportation
   _____ After-school child care
   _____ Special education programs
   _____ Tutoring programs
   _____ Homebound instruction
   _____ Psychological services
   _____ Guidance department

CHAPTER 4

IN-DEPTH EVALUATION
OF SCHOOLS

Once you've absorbed the information in the school's printed materials, it will be time to decide whether you feel the school's educational goals and methods of achieving them coincide with your own goals for your children and the way you'd like them to be taught. If you're pleased with what you've read, or if you're just not sure, call the school and make arrangements to spend a day there—or a good part of one—to tour the entire school and attend some classes. Make arrangements, too, for your children to spend the day attending classes and participating in school activities. Good schools encourage such visits by prospective students—even kindergartners.

Make appointments for private interviews with the principal and some of the teachers who may work with your children. Try to have lunch in the cafeteria and chat with students. Remember, though, poorer quality schools with insecure staffs seldom permit tours or class visits that might expose their deficiencies. There is no point insisting on your "rights" as a prospective parent. Simply look for better schools elsewhere. Schools that are secure about their educational standards are not only proud to display their facilities to visitors, they encourage such visits and even assign students to lead guided tours. That's true at most fine private secondary schools and colleges, where student-led tours provide a wonderful opportunity to get a student's eye view of the school. By all means encourage your children to ask their own questions as you tour. They'll think of some you might overlook, and they'll see how strongly you feel about good education.

As your day progresses, you'll obviously find yourself repeating the same questions to a lot of different people, and that's as it should be. By the end of the day, you should know all about the school and whether to send your children there.

School Facilities

The order of your day is immaterial. I preferred touring before the formal interviews with teachers and the principal because the tour itself often answered many questions while provoking others I hadn't thought of. By touring after the interviews, I always had to make follow-up telephone calls to get new questions answered.

By all means, take a notebook and plenty of pencils. Use one set of pages for evaluation notes and another set to jot down questions to ask the principal later. Make copies of the Report Cards in Part II to "grade" the facilities as you tour. The cards will save you a lot of note taking, because all you'll have to do is put a checkmark under "Above Average, "Satisfactory" or "Inferior" as you view each part of the school. The Report Cards also give you most of the important questions to ask.

As you did on your first visit, look carefully at the physical condition of the exteriors and interiors of all buildings. Second looks often turn up things not noticed the first time. Are they attractive, well maintained, clean? Look once more for adequate safety precautions. How's the interior temperature? And what are students doing? Is the atmosphere quiet and scholarly during class time? Are children wearing happy faces? Double check all your findings from your first cursory visit.

Elementary School

If you visit a kindergarten or preschool class, check for overcrowding and adequate staffing—no more than 20 students per teacher. Is the room stuffy? How does it smell? Do the kindergarten teachers allow the children to go to the bathroom often? Is the classroom well lit and well furnished, with chairs and tables designed to fit small children comfortably?

A kindergarten classroom, remember, is different from other school rooms. It should be much larger, with a wide, open central space and a half-dozen or more learning areas spread around the perimeter of the room. Tables and chairs must be movable and light enough for little children to carry and rearrange in clusters according to the activity. Check that the room has an in-class library with at least 10 or more books for each child. There should be a piano, plenty of blocks, educational toys, art supplies and other materials for learning reading and writing, mathematics, science, music and art and for participating in dramatic play. Many schools also begin integrating computers into daily learning activities in kindergarten. The room should have a happy look and be decorated with children's creative works. A room that's too neat may be a sign that children are not allowed to use the materials enough. A messy room, on the other hand, may be an indication of chaos and lack of teacher control. Neither condition provides much fun or learning. Watch the teacher interact with the children. Kindergarten teachers must be friendly, warm and understanding, without ever losing an opportunity to introduce some learning in every exchange with every child. Be sure to let your children join the class if they're willing. (Don't be surprised, though, if they're fearful and weepy and cling to you.)

Check bathrooms and coat rooms. Are they neat, clean and safe? Are younger children segregated from older ones to prevent bullying? Check the playground to see that it's attractive, safe and big enough for children to run and climb and that it has enough equipment for all the children. Are too many children waiting in lines or idle with nothing to do? A well-run school sees that all children are active on the playground and spend their pent-up energies. Check the gym for adequacy as a bad-weather substitute. Again, it's important that younger children be segregated from older children who might bully or harm them.

Look for many of the same things in first and second grade classes. There should be some expansion of in-class libraries and fewer playthings. You should see some calculators, computers and word processors. First and second grade classrooms are smaller, but the perimeter of the room should still be organized into neat learning areas. Again, rooms should have a happy look and display children's art works as well as serious study projects. There should be more evidence of schoolwork than in kindergarten. Desks and chairs should still be movable so they can be rearranged as needed.

Third and fourth grade classrooms should show evidence of increasing seriousness and study. The perimeter of the room should still be divided into learning areas, but desks may be fixed to the floor, as schools begin to demand that students sit and study for longer periods of time. At this age, too, instead of studying every subject with a single teacher, students may switch to other, special classrooms with teacher-specialists to study music, art or science. The homeroom teacher can then concentrate on reading, writing, arithmetic, history and geography. If computers have not already been integrated into daily learning activities, third grade is the latest grade for the process to begin. Look for another elementary school if you don't see third graders familiarizing themselves with computers. Every student needs to begin learning to operate computers at an early age to assure access to a learning resource as vital as a dictionary or encyclopedia.

Middle School and High School

On a tour of middle schools or high schools, check again that there are enough desks and chairs for all the students—and that they fit. Check, too, that there are adequate teaching supplies and materials. For example, history and geography classes should have sets of oversized wall maps that pull down like window shades, and even the most elementary science classes should have an abundance of equipment for teachers and students to use in conducting experiments that illustrate what students are learning. In other words, it should look like a laboratory and excite students.

Special Use Areas

Check that high school science laboratories have a work area, or "bench," for each student (certainly no more than two to a bench) and enough materials and supplies to perform complete, individual experiments that illustrate what they're studying. Each bench should have functioning burners or alcohol lamps and adequate laboratory glassware—tubing, test tubes, beakers. The lab supply cabinet should be stocked with chemicals for student experiments. Take time to watch a lab class in action.

Visit the library or, as it's often called, the media center. By third grade, children should know how to use a library and should have access to it. Regardless of the level of school, see that it has an up-to-date reference section (check dates of encyclopedia and yearbooks). How many periodicals are in stock? How many volumes are there? Minimum standards of accrediting commissions call for 10 volumes per student with no less than 2,500 books in elementary school libraries and at least 10 volumes per student and no less than 4,000 books in middle school and high school libraries. The library should also have adequate copying facilities and, at the middle and high school levels, data retrieval equipment (microfiche) for encyclopedias and other reference works and for such newspapers as *The New York Times*. It should also have access to other libraries via computer hookup. Check, too, on hours of operation and student access. Even the best library is worthless if it doesn't give students free access to its books and facilities.

Visit the computer lab to see how many units the school has to serve the student body. How often do students get to use computers and for what purposes? Ask, too, whether the school has a writing center.

Visit the art, music and drama areas to check on the number and condition of musical instruments, music stands, the stage and backstage equipment. Are there private practice rooms? Look at the variety of materials and media available in art rooms. What works in progress are evident—oils, water colors, sculptures?

Athletic Facilities

Tour all sports facilities to see that they meet the needs of both girls and boys. Good schools offer adequate facilities for intramural as well as varsity and junior varsity programs for both girls and boys. The vast majority of students cannot make the varsity or junior varsity teams, and they have just as much right to participate in sports as more gifted athletes.

How many sports are there? Depending on its size and location, a good school should offer not less than six and usually nine or ten sports—football, soccer, field hockey and cross-country running in the fall, basketball, wrestling and swimming or ice hockey in winter and baseball, tennis, track and field and possibly lacrosse in spring.

As you tour, see if the playing fields and track are well maintained and safe looking. Is the pool clean and constantly supervised? Are gym facilities well maintained and, once again, safe? Are locker rooms adequate for all participants? Does each youngster have an individual locker? Are lockers in good repair? Can students feel secure about storing valuables in lockers? Is there a separate locker room for visiting teams? Are there adequate, clean showers and changing room facilities? Are boys and girls carefully segregated? Ask if there is an athletic trainer and whether coaches are trained to give first aid. Find out whether a medically trained person attends athletic events. Ask coaches of girls' sports whether they have equal access to all facilities or whether boys' teams have priorities. Can girls field teams and participate in as many sports as boys? Throughout the athletic complex, check to see that there are facilities and possibly an "adaptive gym center" for students with handicaps or health problems. Handicapped students have just as much right to the facilities as the rest of the student body. Addressing this right is an indication that the school cares for all its students and their individual needs. Such caring usually shows up in every other sector of school life, including academics.

As you explore the school, look carefully at all trophy cases and student banners on hallway walls to find out whether sports are emphasized more than (and perhaps at the expense of) academics. Are there any awards for academic competition and achievement, or does every trophy, medal and ribbon relate to sports? Ask teachers whether they feel sports are emphasized over academics. Studies sponsored by the U.S. Department of Education found that academically superior schools offer students as many or more incentives and rewards for academic accomplishments as they do for athletic accomplishments.

Extracurricular Activities

A school information booklet should list available extracurricular activities. Ask to see the facilities for each—the newspaper and yearbook offices, the radio and television station, if there is one, the stage facilities for drama and music presentations, the music rooms and instruments and facilities for photography and any other activities the school may sponsor. Ask about academic extracurricular activities, such as the chess club or science club, and ask about student government to see if the school is training youngsters how to govern themselves responsibly.

A rich mix of extracurricular activities can be as important to high school education as formal academics. Academic clubs, for example, allow students to extend their interests in a particular area beyond the classroom—and without the pressures of preparing for tests. Activities such as drama, singing, band, orchestra and editing and publishing teach valuable skills that are seldom taught in classrooms.

Visit the cafeteria and nurse's office to see whether both appear adequate to meet student needs. Are they clean? Does a peek—and whiff—in the cafeteria whet your appetite? Does the nurse in the health office inspire confidence?

And finally, look at the main locker area. Again, your children will be storing many valuables there. Are they in good repair and safe?

THE FACULTY

As you tour each area of the school you'll be asking questions of faculty and students you meet along the way. Remember, most will be on the job, at work. Save the most profound, searching questions for formal interviews with the principal and individual teachers during their free periods or after school.

Throughout the day, however, keep asking faculty and students, "What's it like teaching here?" and "What's it like going to school here?"—to get a general impression of teacher and student morale.

The most successful schools try to provide teachers with a safe, professional environment that makes it easy for them to do their jobs properly. Surveys in schools across the United States find the happiest, most successful teachers are those with the most authority and responsibility for the education process—design of the curriculum, selection of textbooks, peer evaluation, budget recommendations for their courses and their departments, retention and promotion of students and student discipline. And that's as it should be. After all, good teachers are no different from other skilled professionals. As every study of the best schools has proved, good teachers want to participate in decisions that affect their work, and they want reasonable autonomy in carrying out their responsibilities. They want adequate rewards in the form of professional recognition, promotions and pay increases; they want a pleasant, safe and adequately sized workplace; and they want to be treated with dignity and respect.

Studies funded by the U.S. Department of Education found that America's most successful public schools all give teachers "a great deal of autonomy in doing their work" and that such autonomy, in turn, "produces respect, dignity, deference and esteem . . . (from) colleagues, students and community members." What these studies found, moreover—and this is why teacher autonomy is so important to you as a parent—is that students function better and are more attentive in schools where they know their teachers have authority and are indeed in charge.

Teaching Conditions

So teacher input in academic affairs and student discipline is a key area to probe whenever you have the chance to talk with teachers. You'll want to find out how much time they spend teaching and how much they spend on administrative paperwork. Bloated bureaucracies and mountains of paperwork have crushed education in thousands of schools across the United States. A recent study found one high school administration office processing *45 pounds* of documents a day, with some teachers forced to handle dozens of forms daily—to report on students, to report on their own activities and to replace everything from desk chairs to chalk. Many dedicated teachers have to use class time to fill out forms while students busy themselves at their desks reading materials that should be assigned as homework or simply doing nothing. So find out about the paperwork burden. Ask also whether teachers are saddled with menial tasks such as policing lunchrooms. Top-quality schools do not ask teachers to do anything but teach—no more than four and often only three classes a day. Such schools give every teacher at least one hour a day to meet privately with individual students and at least another full hour a day to prepare lesson plans and grade papers. Top-quality schools also give teachers a comfortable, private lounge area in which to discuss mutual problems with colleagues, and they give teachers their own individual classrooms with desks of their own to store and lock materials and personal effects. In the best schools, all department chairpeople have private offices, and other offices are available to the rest of the faculty to share.

Teacher Input

As you tour, ask teachers what they consider their most serious problems, and find out how much input they have in solving them. If the answer is, "I send problem children to the principal," you know you're dealing with an inadequate teacher and, if you hear the answer too often, an inadequate faculty with little or no authority.

Check on teacher sensitivity and love for youngsters by watching them interact with students in and out of the classroom. See how they react to the little anxieties and problems so many children in early grades bring to school each day. In the higher grades, see if they seem aware of the dangers facing young adolescents. In every class, try to assess the atmosphere. Is the class orderly, tense, quiet? Are students and teachers interested, enthusiastic or bored? What are students doing: drills, taking tests, doing homework assignments, discussing, debating, listening to a lecture or simply doing busy work? After visiting each class, enter the results for each teacher on Report Card No. 7 for teacher evaluations.

As you chat with individual teachers, try also to get a broad evaluation of teaching conditions at the school and the quality of the rest of the faculty (for Report Card No. 6). Ask how much input they have in academic affairs, such as setting the goals and rules of the school. Can the teachers state those goals clearly? How much input do they have in drawing up the curriculum, designing lesson plans, deciding how many and which students will be in their classes? How many students are there in each class? How much choice did teachers have in deciding which courses and which grades they're teaching, and do all teachers teach subjects in which they majored at college? How many college courses did they take in the subjects they're teaching? Are they qualified to teach those courses? Where did they go to college? Were the colleges accredited (check *Barron's Profiles of American Colleges*)? Where did they rank in their graduating classes? Did they do any graduate work? Where else have they taught?

Ask whether the school rewards or honors the best teachers? Good schools do, and many teachers at such schools willingly boast about how competitive their school's salaries are and the low turnover rate high salaries produce. High salaries also lure high percentages of teachers with master's degrees.

"People want to belong to this faculty," said the principal of a high school recognized as "exemplary" in a study called "The Search for Successful Secondary Schools" funded by the U.S. Department of Education. "When a vacancy occurs, there are 40 to 50 applicants."

In addition to monetary rewards and frequent recognitions, such as "teacher of the month" and "teacher of the year," many of the best schools honor their most successful, experienced teachers with the title "Master Teacher." A master teacher must earn that status (and the higher pay that goes with it) by displaying exceptional teaching skills. Be sure, at some point, to find out the school's pay scale and compare it with teacher salaries in other schools in the state and nation. Ask how long the average teacher has taught at the school and what the teacher turnover rate is each year. The best schools have turnover rates of less than 4% a year. Another key question is teacher absenteeism. At the best schools, teacher attendance is better than 95%, thus reducing the disruptions (and extra salary costs) caused by substitute teachers. Too many substitute teachers, no matter how good they are, can disrupt almost any course.

You'll also need to know if discipline and student misbehavior are problems at the school. Do they interfere with the teaching process? Are drugs, alcohol, theft and violence serious problems? Are teachers and students in any physical danger? Top-quality schools leave day-to-day discipline to teachers, but they do not let it become a burden. They simply remove continually disruptive high-risk students from classrooms and the main stream of student life and allow specially trained teachers to deal with them in special settings elsewhere.

Teaching Methods

For years, the world of education has been debating the pro's and con's of "student-centered" and "subject-centered" teaching methods. At one extreme, a student-centered classroom appears to be in chaos, with students unfettered by discipline and permitted to do whatever they choose, while harried teachers try to channel every student's urge into a learning experience.

At the other extreme, a subject-centered setting sees silent, well-dressed, well-groomed youngsters listening intently and unquestioningly to the teacher and, if they're old enough, scribbling notes as quickly as they can. Not until the teacher calls for questions does a student raise his hand. Violation of classroom rules is met with immediate rebuke (and sometimes humiliation) in early grades and, in later years, dismissal from the room and instructions to report to the principal's office. Repeated violations result in parents being called to school.

Even at the kindergarten level, a subject-centered setting sees teachers in complete control with children quietly engaged in individual or group projects. All talk between children is in whispers. When the teacher calls the class together, no student may talk without first raising a hand. The emphasis is on discipline and listening.

If neither extreme sounds appealing, it's because they both are more concerned with student behavior than with learning—and it's questionable how much learning takes place in either setting or how much joy of learning is imparted to the children. Few good schools would advocate either extreme. The best schools try to borrow the best of both teaching methods, and that's what you should look for—an appropriate mix of both methods. With younger children especially, good teachers rely on both approaches. It's important that children's imaginations have free rein from time to time, but it's just as important for them to learn self-discipline.

In general, younger children require more of the child-centered approach. They simply do not have the attention span for a pure, subject-centered approach to education. That's for university lecture halls. On the other hand, as youngsters reach adolescence, a more subject-centered approach is needed to teach some concepts. By the time they reach 15 or 16, students should have the self-discipline to sit in a classroom and concentrate on what a teacher has to say. Even at the high school level, however, skilled teachers use many student-centered teaching methods—asking questions, provoking lively student discussions and leading students along the path to discovery.

So look for and ask about teaching methods. Some student-centered teaching is important, but so is some of the discipline of a subject-centered setting, and the mix should shift as students grow older. Little or no learning of any lasting value takes place in the chaos of a classroom of screaming children hurling every object within reach—except perhaps to duck and run for cover.

Is Learning Taking Place?

Be certain to include enough time on your visit to sit through 20 or more minutes of several classes, if the school permits. Depending on your children's ages, sit in classes of different grades in an elementary school or in different courses in a middle school or high school. Watch at all times whether real learning is taking place. Little learning is going on if there is no joy or excitement on the faces of the children, regardless of the complexity of the subject matter, or if they are inattentive and not actively participating in the classroom process, asking and responding to tough questions that make them use their minds as well as memories. Real learning, according to one educator, only takes place as children learn to think critically and make discoveries.

The student—not the teacher—must be the most active participant in the learning process. The teacher is merely a leader—asking questions, provoking students to ask questions and guiding students to correct answers by getting them to look things up and to do experiments of their own. Regardless of age, everyone learns best by doing. Good teachers encourage even the youngest children in kindergarten to do things—to touch, handle, count and interrelate materials. The more senses and faculties involved, the more learning takes place. When kindergarten youngsters say aloud that three blocks are more than two while handling the blocks, they are using four faculties—speaking, hearing, seeing and feeling. Moreover, they are unconsciously experiencing the interconnection between language skills and math. Far more learning takes place in doing than in silent staring at a sheet of paper with pictures of blocks and a place to make a pencil mark to answer the printed question, "Which set is bigger?"

At a more advanced stage, student-centered teaching encourages teacher-supervised projects and, later, in high school, independent research projects. All are designed to help students learn by doing. Even in advanced high school science (and college) classes, students conduct their own experiments to prove or disprove the theories they study in their textbooks. Students learn far more by measuring the speed of sound themselves than by being forced to memorize: "Sound travels in air at about 1090 feet per second at 0° C (32° F) or 1130 feet per second at 20° C (68° F). It travels 4.5 times faster in water and 15 times faster in steel."

So watch carefully how teachers interact with students and how much time is spent questioning students, leading them rather than talking at them. Indirect questions that require thoughtful responses ("How would you solve this problem?") are usually better than direct questions requiring rote answers. See if the teachers motivate students with praise and encouragement rather than criticism. And note carefully how much time teachers spend "talking at" the students. If most of the class is devoted to lecturing or, worse, to school announcements, attendance taking and discipline, little learning is taking place, and that classroom, at least, can hardly be classed top-quality.

Listen, too, to determine if teachers interconnect the knowledge from different disciplines. Failure to connect knowledge gleaned in one classroom with knowledge from others diminishes the amount of learning that takes place in all classes. Indeed, teachers in the best middle and high schools work closely together as teams to involve students in cross-disciplinary projects. A seventh grade study of ancient Egyptian civilization, for example, would not only involve the history teacher, it would involve the math teacher (for the geometry of pyramids and cubes), the science teacher (for the principles and mathematics of levers and pulleys), and the English teacher (for the significance of hieroglyphics in the development of languages and for grammar, writing and rhetorical skills for written and oral reports). Even the art teacher would join the team to teach students illustration techniques for their reports and explain the significance of Egyptian art in the history of art.

A 12-year-old who studies (and visualizes) the mechanical advantage of levers and pulleys in cross-disciplinary studies of this type learns far more than a youngster forced simply to memorize the isolated formula, Weight × Distance = Weight × Distance.

As you tour classrooms, be sure to look at the quality, age and number of materials available for teaching, including textbooks. Average public school spending on textbooks and other instructional materials has dropped an astonishing 50% over the past 25 years. Good schools have enough up-to-date textbooks for all the children so that they do not have to share. Look on the reverse side of textbook title pages for copyright dates. Is the teacher using out-of-date books and if so, why? A recent study found that more than half the elementary school science textbooks in U.S. public schools are out of date. Is the use of out-of-date textbooks consistent throughout the school? (The copyright dates are, of course, less important for story books in the early grades and literature for older children.) Check the table of contents of textbooks to see that they cover all the material students should be learning in that class. Use Part III, The Academic Curriculum, as a guide, and ask teachers whether they do indeed cover the material.

While visiting classes, watch also whether bells and loudspeaker announcements constantly interrupt the teaching process. No good school interrupts valuable classroom time with announcements or end-of-period bells that might cut a teacher off in mid-sentence. A well-organized school administration jealously guards classtime for teaching and makes certain that all announcements are made at the beginning of the day during assembly or homeroom.

Watch also whether classroom time is flexible or not. In addition to absence of bells, many of the most successful middle and high schools have abandoned rigid time schedules. Instead, they divide days into time modules (usually 20 minutes each). Using interdisciplinary team teaching methods, teachers in each team plan and coordinate the week's lessons and assign an appropriate number of time modules to each class for each day of the week, depending on what the team is teaching. Thus, the science teacher might need 80 minutes on one day to teach mathematical concepts involved in moving huge blocks of stone to build the Pyramids. The history teacher might need more time on another day to teach about Egyptian civilization; the English teacher would need more than the usual modules on another day to teach the significance of hieroglyphics in the development of written languages. The math teacher would need extra modules on still another day to teach the geometry of the Pyramids, and the art teacher would certainly want a chance to teach Egyptian art forms. So, from day to day and week to week, the teaching team determines which discipline will dominate the schedule at any given time.

The effects of team teaching on children of all ages can be remarkable, because it allows them to pursue knowledge at a pace determined by requirements of the subject rather than by bells. In conventional classrooms, students can lose five minutes or more of each 40- or 50-minute period settling into their seats at the beginning of the period and an equal amount at the end, gathering their things in anticipation of the bell—which often interrupts teachers in mid-sentence and sets off a mad student scramble to the door.

Now, just because a school does not practice team teaching does not mean it is not an outstanding school. There is little need for team teaching in kindergarten or the early elementary years, when a single teacher should have a broad enough store of knowledge to provide true interdiciplinary instruction. And that's the key here—interdiciplinary instruction, with or without teaching teams.

But ask about team teaching—certainly at middle schools and high schools. If you find a school that uses the approach, sign your kids up! If it's not standard practice, ask if it's used once in a while or if teachers in each grade at least coordinate their course curricula and lesson plans to assure solid interdisciplinary instruction. If the faculty or principal denigrate the practice, that *may* indicate they're behind the times.

Finally, don't forget to ask teachers about tracking, or homogeneous grouping. More and more good schools are abandoning the practice in favor of heterogeneous grouping, which mixes gifted and average students in the same classes. Studies show that heterogeneous grouping not only pulls up the average achievement of the class, it pulls up achievement levels for every individual in the class. Even the slowest children make far more progress when mixed with abler youngsters, who become role models for the rest of the class and create peer pressures to excel academically. Moreover, the gifted children also progress faster—especially when they're given tutoring responsibilities. Pairing children in one-to-one "cooperative learning" relationships helps high achievers expand their understanding of the material as they explain it to their slower partners. Both groups of children grow socially as well as academically by experiencing the statisfactions of working cooperatively with others.

Cooperative learning, of course, does not include children with severe learning impairments. It simply means pairing average seventh graders for example, with quicker seventh graders so they can all progress to the eighth grade together. Severely impaired students obviously need individual attention in specialized classes, and, in such cases, some tracking is necessary, as it may be for some exceptionally gifted children. In other words, abandonment of tracking does not mean abandoning individual attention to every student's special needs. It does, however, mean abandoning the practice of condemning whole groups of children to permanently segregated learning environments in which they must progress at rates predetermined by the average level in each track.

Nonclassroom Faculty

In addition to classroom faculty, try to meet one or more members of the guidance staff, athletic department and faculty in charge of extra-curricular activities. There will, of course, be some and perhaps total overlap, and you might ask (as diplomatically as possible) whether teachers have to assume obligations in nonacademic areas against their wishes. Good schools don't force teachers to take on nonacademic duties they don't enjoy.

In each area, ask what training the faculty advisor or coach had in the activity. Although extracurricular activities and sports are "fun," they are also important learning experiences, and those who teach should be as skilled in teaching and have as strong a background in such activities as teachers in courses such as mathematics.

Guidance Office

The guidance office in most U.S. public high schools is one of the greatest sources of frustration for the average student. It also produces unnecessary conflicts between parents and the school and parents and their children. Millions of parents routinely tell their children to "ask your guidance counselor" for authoritative answers to questions about curriculum, career choices and college admissions procedures. Unfortunately, what parents seldom realize is that the *average* high school guidance counselor has 420 youngsters to counsel—not only on curriculum, career choices and college admissions procedures, but on sex, pregnancy, prenatal care, drug abuse, parental abuse, conflicts at home, parental divorce, death, poor school grades, misbehavior, crime and endless other problems.

So it is virtually impossible for the average high school student to see a guidance counselor on the spur of the moment for help in solving an immediate problem. At best, the student may get an appointment a week later and seldom for more than five minutes. When youngsters report these difficulties to parents, the latter either don't believe their children tried hard enough to see the guidance counselors or they call up the school and are themselves drawn into a conflict. All of which is why the best private schools usually don't even have guidance departments. Instead, they assign each student a faculty advisor to serve as an adult friend and advocate in the school, and they hire one or more specialists in college admissions procedures to handle that aspect of guidance counseling.

So, in evaluating even the finest schools, look for other services from the guidance department—services they are realistically able to render. Ask, for example, whether the office provides contacts with college representatives and with career-advisory organizations such as Junior Achievement, Future Homemakers of America, Future Farmers of America, the Boy Scouts of America's Career Explorers program or the Business and Professional Women's Association.

Ask also whether each student's complete school record is always available on request. It's important for all parents to exercise their rights once a year under the Family Educational Rights and Privacy Act of 1974 (called the Buckley Amendment) to review their children's educational records. You as a parent have the right under federal law to review your child's confidential educational file to see that it contains no malicious or false material. You have the right to insist upon the removal of such material. If there is a negative report that is accurate, you have the right to insert an explanation of any extenuating circumstances that may have provoked the report (for example, your child may have misbehaved in response to the death of a loved one).

Be certain, therefore, that those who staff the guidance office are aware of your rights as a parent. But don't expect much guidance for your children, and don't conclude that the school is not strong academically because its guidance staff is overwhelmed. Few public schools have large enough guidance departments, and many of the strongest schools academically have too few guidance counselors. Indeed, a guidance department would need one counselor for every 15 to 20 students to satisfy growing community demands for schools to assume child-rearing responsibilities that properly belong to parents. That would double school costs. Schools in the United States are having enough difficulties educating children, and it's unfair of parents to expect them to do more than that. Guidance departments cannot and will not provide surrogate parents—or surrogate psychiatrists, for that matter. What they can and should do is provide one or more specialists in key areas such as career counseling and college admissions. They should also be able to refer parents to psychological counselors in the community.

A good guidance department should also have a large, well stocked library of books and brochures on all topics of interest to adolescents (careers, college admissions, sexuality, chemical substance abuse and adolescent behavior problems) along with plentiful supplies of whatever forms students might need for applying for jobs or admission to colleges or taking college entrance examinations.

Knowing that no guidance department can afford a staff large enough for close one-to-one relationships with every student, many quality public high schools are now copying what private schools do by assigning a faulty advisor to every student as well as a guidance counselor. This gives every student a competent, thoughtful, caring adult advocate in school to consult about curriculum choices, college admissions and personal problems.

It's important to realize, however, that you, as a parent, must be your children's ultimate guidance counselor. No one will be willing to do as thorough and caring a job as you. If you're not familiar with college entrance requirements and the college admissions process, there are ample books on the subject, many of them relatively short and easy to read, including my own book, *A Student's Guide to College Admissions—Everything Your Guidance Counselor Has No Time to Tell You* (Facts On File, 1990). Career counseling is equally simple to learn. Every two years the U.S. Department of Labor puts out an authoritative "Occupational Outlook Handbook," which should be available in the school's guidance office or, if not, at a major public library. You can also buy it from the U.S. Government Printing Office in Washington, D.C.

CHECKLIST
In-depth Evaluation of Schools

School Facilities (Report Card No. 8)
□ Academic facilities
___ Classrooms
___ Specialized classrooms (science labs, music rooms, etc.)
___ Library (media center)
□ Nonacademic facilities
___ Hallways
___ Bathrooms
___ Playgrounds
___ Athletics
___ Gymnasium
___ Playing fields
___ Changing rooms/showers
___ Extracurricular facilities

Faculty (Report Cards No. 4, 5, 6, 7)
□ Academic
___ Teaching conditions
___ Teacher input/authority
___ Teacher rewards
___ Paperwork versus teaching

—— Classroom interruptions
—— Major teacher problems
—— Teaching methods
    —— Class atmosphere (teacher-student rapport)
    —— Is learning taking place?
    —— Student-centered versus subject-centered approaches
    —— Critical thinking (does teacher lead or lecture?)
    —— Interdisciplinary and/or team teaching
    —— Tracking
    —— Textbooks (age and number)
☐ Nonclassroom faculty
—— Athletics
    —— Teaching skills and training
    —— First aid training
—— Extracurricular activities
—— Guidance

CHAPTER 5

A VISIT WITH THE PRINCIPAL AND TEACHERS

Study after study has found that a school's success is directly related to the principal's competence and degree of autonomy and authority. The principal, in other words, should be the most important person in any school and the most important person for you to meet and talk to at length to get authoritative answers to all your unanswered questions, especially questions about school policy and the quality of the academic program. The principal's frankness with you will in itself be an indication of the quality of education in the school.

A good principal should be able to articulate clearly the specific goals of the school, and that's the first question to ask—to see if they coincide with your own educational goals for your children. Once the principal has made the school's goals clear, try to get his or her assessment of the school. How close is it to accomplishing those goals? Ask about the school's strong points and weak points. Find out what the principal considers the school's outstanding characteristics and its major problems. What is the principal's vision for the future? Is there any new program that truly excites the principal? What worries the principal most? If the answers all involve winning or losing athletic teams, look for another school!

Test the principal's awareness of the problems and dangers children of all ages face today, and ask every question you can think of that teachers, students and printed materials left unanswered.

Probe deeply into the question of teacher authority and the principal's own authority. Who runs the school—the principal and teachers or the school superintendent and school board? As stated earlier, every study of U.S. schools has found student achievement highest where principals and teachers control education and school boards limit their functions to broad policy and budgetary oversight. Where learning is the primary goal of a community, that community and its school board give educators the job and authority to educate youngsters without interference. So, before enrolling your children in any school, find out whether their education will be in the hands of professional educators or not. Ask again about the degree of principal and faculty authority over teacher evaluation, hiring and firing, determination of budget needs, design of curriculum, selection of textbooks, student discipline and student retention and promotion. (Good schools, by the way, do not promote children who fail. They make them repeat the work in special, smaller classes in summer school to try to help them catch up and rejoin their agemates.)

Ask, too, about the frequency and length of parent-teacher conferences and parent-principal conferences, the ease or difficulty of having such meetings and the authority of a teacher or the principal to solve problems on the spot. Ask about the difficulty of switching from one course to another if, for example, children simply cannot handle a subject such as chemistry or have been placed in too easy or difficult a level in a subject. And ask about the difficulty of switching teachers if you or your children are dissatisfied or don't get along with a teacher.

Ask the principal whether the school is accredited. If not, why not? What is it about accreditation standards that makes it too difficult for the school to earn accreditation? Again, don't confuse accreditation with state certification. If the school is unaccredited, has it at least had a curriculum audit by the American Association of School Administrators (see Chapter 2)? If not, why not? Ask about the faculty's average length of stay. If it's less than five years, find out why. They're probably unhappy about something. If they've been there an average of 10 years or more, that's a sign of a happy school environment.

Ask any other questions you feel were left unanswered by the printed materials and tour of the school. The principal is the one person who should have all the answers. If that's not the case, look for another school.

Probe into the principal's own academic background and training for the job. The principal's credentials should be on the office walls. Most accreditation associations require principals to have at least a master's degree. Make sure both the bachelor's and master's degrees and any other degrees are from accredited colleges and universities (look in *Barron's Profiles of American Colleges*) and not from "diploma mills." Find out where the principal worked before and whether he or she still teaches. The best principals try to keep a foot "in the trenches" by teaching at least once in a while to stay in day-to-day contact with faculty and student problems.

ACADEMIC QUALITY

Expect the principal's answers to be relatively optimistic. After all, the principal is the "boss"—the school's primary public representative and, ultimately, responsible for conditions in the school. To admit that a school is inferior reflects on the principal's own performance (although one middle school principal once admitted to me he and the faculty were unable to control student violence. Obviously, I took my son to another school!).

So, in trying to assess educational quality, avoid questions a principal can answer with sweeping generalizations such as, "Our students can stand up with the best." And don't pay much attention to achievement and state competency tests. State competency tests, which are required for high school diplomas in more than 30 states, often barely measure literacy and can be childishly simple. A question on one such test for *high school students* lists telephone numbers for the fire department, police department, doctor, ambulance, F.B.I. and Coast Guard and asks the student to check the number to call for a flu shot.

As for most so-called "achievement tests," high scores seldom measure actual achievement unless they are administered by independent agencies with no ties to schools whose children take the tests. Given to children of all ages starting in elementary school, such tests are often produced by the states themselves. Questions remain the same or similar from year to year, and teachers can use the previous year's questions to prepare students to get high scores.

Don't be surprised, therefore, at the high scores principals can cite for their schools. There are enough kinds of achievement tests around for any school to produce high scores. So find out what kind of achievement tests are given and who administers them. If independently administered, they may be of some value. In top quality elementary and middle schools, 85% of all students should score at or above grade level on such tests.

However, any principal that talks more about test scores than about learning may be sending a signal that valuable classroom time at the school is spent learning test-taking techniques and memorizing the previous year's test answers instead of acquiring knowledge.

So, ask about student achievement, but base questions primarily on the appropriate sections in Part III of this book, The Academic Curriculum. Get exact descriptions of what each grade or course covers and compare that to the standards in Part III. Ask for details of student academic achievements in each grade.

The best test scores to use for evaluating high schools are the PSAT, SAT and ACT college admissions tests, which are given by independent outside administrators to juniors and seniors. Although not designed for the purpose, these tests can serve as a good measure of high school quality if enough students at a school take them. So ask for the school's average PSAT, SAT and ACT scores if they were not available in a school profile. Ask what percentage of the previous year's senior class took SAT or ACT tests and what percentage went on to four-year colleges.

The Core Curriculum

Except for the need to conduct teacher interviews in greater depth, academic evaluation techniques for elementary schools do not differ much from those you'll use at middle schools or high schools. The curriculum obviously lies at the heart of academic quality, and top quality schools in the United States now require *all* children of *all ages* to study a core curriculum. The principal should be able to explain the core curriculum of the school and the goals of that curriculum—to teach students the ability to think critically, to understand the connections between different disciplines, to learn as well as test successfully, to develop a healthy way of life and to be an active citizen.

The core curriculum, which should begin in kindergarten and extend through high school, teaches knowledge and skills in seven academic subjects: English language (rhetoric as well as reading and writing), mathematics (including computer science), social studies (history, geography and civics), science, modern foreign languages (starting no later than fourth grade), fine arts and health (including physical education). In addition, many leading schools have now added an adjunct activity to the core curriculum—public service, which is described below.

Leading educators believe the core curriculum constitutes a basic education essential for *every* child—not just those who will eventually go to college. The core curriculum fills almost all class time in elementary and middle school and the first two years of high school (see Part III, especially Figure 3 in Chapter 7, Figure 4 in Chapter 8, and Figure 5 in Chapter 9). In the last two years of high school, when students begin to have a choice of electives in advanced academic, business or vocational courses, the core curriculum should account for about half the work, with electives making up the rest of their curriculum.

Specific descriptions for each course in the core curriculum for every grade are in Part III. Here, though, in broad terms, is what the core curriculum looks like:

1. *English (language arts)*. No one can function without mastery of language and communications skills, regardless of the work they choose

as adults. A primary objective of every quality school in the United States is to teach students to read well and accurately and to write clearly and effectively. If you see that this is not the primary objective of principals you interview—if they only mention it as an afterthought after prodding from you—the school is probably not very good. Almost half of all fourth graders and one-third of all eighth graders write fewer than 12 papers during the whole school year in all subjects combined—which is why illiteracy has become one of the most acute problems of American youth. It should be uppermost in the minds of every teacher, school principal and educator worthy of those titles.

In the early school years, kindergarten through third grade, good schools teach students basic reading, writing (including penmanship) and speaking and listening skills (rhetoric). Most remedial work should be completed during those years as well, although students transferring from a poorer quality school might need to continue remediation an extra year to catch up. Again, Part III gives detailed descriptions of the work for each grade.

As children progress into higher levels of elementary school and middle school, they should gain complete command of and be able to apply the rules of grammar, expand their vocabularies and spelling abilities, be able to write stories and themes of considerable lengths—and be doing so at least once a week! They should also be able to speak before groups of their peers and listen to and understand other student speakers. Rhetoric—the art of speaking and listening—is essential to all functioning human beings; when schools stop teaching it, they risk turning out youngsters incapable of communicating with each other and with the adult world. The unintelligible teenager's desperate effort to speak—"well, ya know, like . . . well, ya know"—is the result of that lack of education, and, sadly, there is no way to know what such a youngster is trying to say. So look for rhetoric as an essential element of English courses in top quality elementary, middle and high schools.

Schools at all levels—even kindergarten—should be using classic literature to teach reading and make it fun. Elementary schools should be using classic children's literature. Middle schools and high schools should be using more complex works by such authors as Aeschylus, Sophocles, Homer, Dickens, Scott, Shakespeare, Keats, Ibsen, Shaw, Brontë, Hawthorne, Hemingway, Fitzgerald, Steinbeck, Miller and other great poets, playwrights, novelists and writers—not Harlequin Romances or books children might select on their own. In addition to basic grammar and composition, outstanding high schools require at least three years of English literature and writing and rhetoric for *every* student, regardless of post-high school educational and career goals. They also require students to read at least one book during every Christmas vacation and three every summer vacation.

2. *Mathematics.* Good school systems require students to study and learn mathematics every year throughout elementary and middle school and to continue through at least two years of high school. "The study of math is . . . a vital component of a good education," says William J. Bennett, former U.S. Secretary of Education. "In part, the study of math is the study of problems and solutions. It builds both the analytic spirit and the deductive capacity on which intelligent thought depends. And it teaches students the value of precise thinking."

Elementary schools should cover all fundamentals of arithmetic—addition, subtraction, multiplication, division, fractions, decimals, percentages, weights and measures and problem solving. Remedial work in math should be completed by the end of sixth grade. Middle and high school math should progress through beginning and intermediate algebra and plane geometry, trigonometry and solid geometry. College-bound students also need precalculus and calculus. Math studies should give every student an ability to understand numbers and quantities and to use them accurately and quickly to solve problems in and out of the classroom. Unfortunately, most U.S. public schools are failing to teach mathematics adequately. Every recent test comparing U.S. elementary school, middle school and high school students with comparable students in Europe and Japan showed U.S. students finishing last in mathematics skills and achievement. But only part of this math illiteracy has been traced to poor teaching. American parents are also responsible because of their prevailing attitude that success in school math is tied to innate abilities—an attitude that excuses poor performance and failure. Japanese and Chinese parents, in contrast, believe that success in math lies in hard work.

The mathematics curriculum in the early years should also teach students mastery of all important technological learning tools, such as calculators and computers.

3. *Social studies (history, geography and civics).* History studies should begin by third grade with local lore and gradually expand into North American and U.S. history and geography. By sixth grade, students should also have learned the geography of the United States and the world. Right now, more than 20% of U.S. 12-year-olds can't even find the United States on a map of the world. Middle schools should require two and high schools three years of history, including ancient and medieval history; the history and changing geography of Western Civilization, of which the United States is a part and derives its own culture; the history and geography of nonwest-

ern civilizations, which dominate the world in terms of land mass and population, and, of course, U.S. history.

In addition to straight-forward history, top quality schools are now reinstituting studies in civics, or political science. Although touched on throughout the elementary years and in various social studies courses, good high schools now require a full year's study of how governments—especially our own local, state and federal governments—function. With fewer than 20% of the eligible population voting in most elections in the United States, educators believe it important to teach students about various political systems, about democracy, about the shaping and operation of our own system and about the political and social issues U.S. citizens face today. Civics need not be taught under that name as a separate course if it is integrated into American and world history courses. The important thing is to find out *whether* it's taught, not how or when.

4. *Science.* Science at every level should teach students how to discover and learn—i.e., the so-called "scientific method," which can be applied to every area of life. Science teaches students of all ages critical thinking and problem solving. It teaches how to gather data, consider cause-and-effect relationships and reach sound conclusions. Science should also teach students how the world functions. Science education should begin in kindergarten and the early grades, when kids view experiments with excitement and teachers can take advantage of their enthusiasm to kindle a life-long interest in science. Unfortunately, public elementary school failure to make science fun is seen as a key reason why less than half of all U.S. high school students take any science courses. Of 24,000 U.S. high schools, more than 7000 offer no physics courses; 4,000 have no chemistry courses; and 2,000 don't even teach biology.

Good elementary and middle schools insist that, by the end of eighth grade, every student has a basic knowledge of biology, zoology, chemistry, physics, geology, astronomy, ecology and evolution and a basic understanding of the interdependency of each of these areas with humankind. At the high school level, the core curriculum should include three years of more advanced studies in biology, physics and chemistry. *Run* from any high school that teaches creation science, involving unscientific Biblical explanations of the creation of the world. The courts have held that such courses overstep the line separating church and state and actually teach religion, not science. The quality of education in such schools is usually at the lowest level.

5. *Foreign languages.* Top-quality schools now begin teaching foreign languages no later than fourth grade. Unfortunately, they constitute less than 25% of U.S. public schools, and even in those schools, less

than half the children actually study foreign languages. No state actually requires high schools even to teach foreign languages, and fewer than 30% of high school students bother to study them. In European and most other countries in the world, all students must study two foreign languages—one for six years, the other for four years.

By the year 2000, the United States will be the world's fifth largest population of Hispanic origin. Spanish is spoken by more people in the world than any other language except Mandarin Chinese, English and Hindi. Few Americans today do not have direct or indirect economic ties to foreign trade. The roots of our own language lie in Latin, Greek and German, and foreign language studies enhance student knowledge and understanding of their own language. That is why the better school systems teach foreign languages every year from fourth through ninth grade and require all students to extend their studies for at least two years in high school.

Many good middle schools also insist on a year's study of "general languages," which teaches origins and meanings of English word roots, suffixes and prefixes and the development of the English language. Not only does such a course teach word meanings and expand student vocabularies and spelling abilities, it teaches students to look at words they've never seen before and work out meanings by analyzing roots, prefixes and suffixes. In effect, it teaches literacy.

6. *Fine Arts.* Just as students must learn the use of verbal symbols to communicate, they must learn the use of nonverbal symbols to become educated adults. The arts are as essential for communication as words, and it is no coincidence that totalitarian societies censor the fine arts as much as they do the written and spoken word. Unfortunately, many states do not even require fine arts studies in school. Studies of the fine arts should begin in kindergarten and continue into the high school years, where a sound core curriculum requires at least one year's formal study of music and another of art for graduation. Studies in the fine arts at different levels should include painting, sculpture, graphic arts, singing, music appreciation, simple composition, instruction in various musical instruments, stage performances and dance, along with a variety of opportunities to experiment, perform, interpret and experience the fine arts.

7. *Health.* From their earliest years, children in top-quality schools are now being taught about the life cycle and how to care for their bodies. At varying ages, they learn about hygiene, dental care, skin care, feelings, mental health, aging and dying, communicable diseases, sexuality, molestation and abuse, and abuse of alcohol, drugs and other chemical substances. Unfortunately, many schools assign

such instruction to physical education teachers who often never studied the field and are not trained to teach it. "Phys Ed" is *not* the same as health education, although many physical education teachers study both. Top-quality schools only permit specialists trained in health education to teach it. So check on the backgrounds of teachers assigned to health ed. It should be taught every year through elementary and middle schools and offered as a one-semester requirement in high school.

8. *Public service.* Usually considered an extracurricular or even an out-of-school activity, public service is becoming an integral part of education in top-quality elementary and middle schools. Indeed, it is a requirement for graduation at some high schools, and many selective colleges and universities give an edge to candidates who have demonstrated a willingness during their high school years to fulfill social and civic obligations through some sort of school or community service. As Harvard University puts it:

We place great value in a candidate's capacity to move beyond the limits of personal achievement to involvement in the life of the community at large. We seek candidates who demonstrate a willingness to take an interest in the lives and welfare of others or to place themselves in situations which call for personal initiative and leadership.

Parents, of course, have the primary responsibility for instilling a sense of responsibility in their children. But educators have long believed that schools must also contribute. Good elementary and middle schools now enlist their students in group projects to help the community. Top-quality high schools also urge students to participate in meaningful public service, either in school or in the community. One survey found that nearly 80% of all high school students do not participate in *any* extracurricular activities at school. The best schools no longer tolerate such inactivity either in school or out. Fulfilling public-service obligations takes many forms, depending on the community. It can mean spending time with lonely elderly people, helping deprived children learn to read, tutoring another student in school, cleaning up litter in parks and streets, working on a school-improvement project or simply participating in important extracurricular activities that contribute to school life—such as student government or student publications. In other words, good schools now expect their students to be responsibly engaged in bettering their school, community and world.

Teaching

After discussing the core curriculum, the principal should also outline the school's approach to teaching. Teaching methods are as important an indication of academic quality as the curriculum.

As mentioned earlier, many top-quality schools now use team-teaching approaches that allow teachers from each discipline to work together to show the connections between the courses they teach and the courses students are studying in other classes. Such teaching teams encourage students to be active in the learning process—to ask questions about interesting phenomena and events and then engage in research and collection of evidence to find answers to those questions.

Asking and helping youngsters discover through their own research why the sun is hot produces far more learning than simply commanding them to memorize the sun's temperature. Good schools, in other words, do not separate knowing from finding out and do emphasize critical thinking and understanding over memorization of facts, figures and technical vocabulary. Any principal that uses the terms "interdisciplinary" and "team teaching" in describing the school's teaching approach is probably running a sound operation.

Open versus Restricted Curriculum

At the high school level, it's important to find out whether the curriculum is "open" or restricted—in other words, how much self-determination students have over course selection. To give adolescents free rein to choose courses and educate themselves is an abdication of adult responsibilities and often borders on neglect. According to the National Center for Education Statistics, non-directed "cafeteria" curricula that allow students to select their own high school courses are closely related to the disgracefully high 27.4% dropout rate in U.S. high schools and an illiteracy rate of 13% among our 17-year-olds. It is the job of parents and educators to educate the young. Teenagers are not wise enough to select what courses to study. Any high school principal who gives students that right is failing them and simply not doing his job. So, in evaluating high schools, the fewer electives the better. Good elementary and middle schools offer students no electives. Good high schools offer none to ninth and tenth graders and limit eleventh and twelth grade electives to no more than 50% of the curriculum. Electives are limited either to advanced academic courses for college-bound students or business and vocational courses for students who plan attending community colleges and technical institutes after high school graduation.

Many weaker schools offer huge "cafeterias" of courses that give youngsters more choices than they can handle. Too many choices allow them to fulfill graduation requirements by taking easy courses. The students graduate with diplomas in their hands but without enough knowledge in their heads to function successfully in college or the job market. As the National Commission on Excellence in Education explained it, "Secondary school curricula have been homogenized, diluted and diffused to the point that they no longer have a central purpose. In effect, we have a cafeteria-style curriculum in which the appetizers and desserts can easily be mistaken for the main courses."

So, it's important to get an idea of the quality of courses offered. What does it mean to take "English," for example? At top-quality schools, English courses will be limited to serious studies of literature and writing at progressively more difficult levels, with little or no choice each year. Weaker schools may offer as many as 30 different "English" courses—some that rely totally on audiovisual equipment and require no independent reading at home. Others involve superficial examinations of "contemporary books," which students can often pick themselves from racks of popular books in drug stores. Top colleges, however, know the value of such courses and do not accept them for credit toward admission.

In evaluating high schools, therefore, it's a good idea to compare the courses offered with those required by the most selective colleges and universities. The courses described in Part III of this book meet those requirements. Use it as your guide.

As your children progress through middle and high school, it's important to monitor their curricula continually to see that it not only meets graduation requirements but also the requirements of all colleges and universities to which they may one day apply. Don't expect a guidance counselor to do the job. In the end, it's a parent's responsibility to see that children are not barred from the best colleges or from the workplace because they took the wrong high school courses.

If your children are college-bound, steer them away from almost all courses that do not appear in the curriculum outlined in Part III. Your children and their friends may well tell you that "everybody's taking" some other course and even assure you that colleges recognize such courses. But if you want your children to have the best possible academic education and be eligible to attend the most selective colleges and universities, use Part III as your guide. If you're in doubt, call the admissions offices of some of the colleges in the top three categories of *Barron's Profiles of American Colleges* and double check. Whatever you do, don't turn to friends and neighbors for advice unless they are professional educators. Use authoritative guides such as *Barron's*.

There are, however, some noncredit courses your children may have to take, such as physical education and health, and other noncredit courses they will want to—and should—take because they will prove useful, even if they don't earn credits towards college admission. Typing, word processing or "keyboarding," as it's now called, is one of these. It's an absolute essential for doing good school work. Indeed, it's a good idea for students to learn typing and word processing in elementary school as soon as they have enough finger dexterity. Their work will go faster and be neater and more accurate. Some good schools require that children learn this skill no later than seventh grade and that they use it to produce papers throughout high school.

At the high school level, driver education is another essential course that does not count toward meeting admission requirements of selective colleges. It does, however, teach youngsters to drive and make them eligible for less costly insurance when they obtain their licenses in most states. (Neither typing nor driver education is mentioned in Part III, which is limited to academic courses.)

Schoolwork and Homework

One reason for the decline in primary and secondary public school education in America has been the decline in the time that students spend studying. A study of the school week by The National Commission on Excellence in Education found that the *average* U.S. public school only provides 22 hours of actual instruction a week. In many schools, students spend as few as 17 hours in class each week. A University of Michigan study found that fifth graders only spend 64% of their school time on academic activities, compared to 87% for Japanese students.

Students spend the rest of their school time in assemblies and other gatherings, listening to special announcements, filling out meaningless forms, participating in sports or extracurricular activities or just "hanging out." Making matters worse is the length of the school day and the school year—typically six hours a day for 180 days a year, or 1080 hours. In contrast, students in England, Japan and other industrialized nations spend 8 hours a day at school, 220 days a year, or 1768 hours— 64% more!

As for homework, two-thirds of U.S. *high school seniors* report having or doing less than 1 hour per night. More than one-fifth of all eleventh graders say they have no homework. And yet, with less studying in and out of school, most public high schools continue reporting *higher* student grades and *higher* scores on state achievement and competency tests—the ones discussed earlier, for which teachers prepare students in advance by studying previous years' tests. Student scores on such tests are bound to improve if the questions remain the same from year to year.

But student scores on tests like the SAT, administered by independent agencies such as the College Board, have not improved. They've declined sharply over the past 30 years. So check on the amount of academic instruction each week and the amount of homework students are expected to do. Homework should extend the school day into every child's evening, so that television viewing is the exception on school nights rather than the rule. A good rule of thumb to determine the *minimum* number of minutes of homework every school should demand from students each weekday night and on the weekend is to multiply the student's grade by 10. Sixth graders should have one hour of homework each night; twelfth graders two hours. For better quality schools, use a factor of 15—one and one-half hours for sixth graders; three hours for twelfth graders, and for the very best schools, use a factor of 20.

In other words, the highest quality schools set the highest standards for their students, require the most work in class and at home and have the highest expectations for their students. Unlike average and substandard schools, they help students adjust to high academic standards rather than adjusting their standards downwards. Like the best Japanese schools, the best U.S. schools believe firmly that hard work rather than innate ability is the basis of student academic achievement. Faculties at such schools reject student arguments (often supported by parents) that "I'll never get this" or "I've never been good at math." Instead, they insist that such students simply work harder until they do "get it."

Honors and Advanced Placement Courses

If you're evaluating high schools, ask the principal about the honors program. Although the course catalog may have listed honors courses, the school may simply be using that designation to disguise a tracking system that relegates vocational and general diploma students to substandard courses. So find out the percentage of students that take honors courses and the percentage of students from those courses admitted to selective colleges and universities. Also find out average SAT and ACT scores of students enrolled in the honors program. Honors courses should be designed to prepare students for selective colleges—not just average colleges. *Every* course in the core curriculum should be designed to prepare students for average colleges. Honors courses should be for advanced students.

In evaluating a high school, it's essential to know whether it offers Advanced Placement (AP) courses and in what subjects. A school without AP courses is probably not setting high standards for its students and could deprive your children of important educational opportunities. Designed by the College Board, AP courses are offered in English composition, European history, American history, Latin, Spanish, French, German, biology, chemistry and physics at most top-quality schools. Advanced Placement courses are the equivalent of freshman college courses and are open only to students who have completed the entire standard high school curriculum in the particular subject. Successful completion of an AP course entitles a student to take a College Board AP exam in the subject. Many colleges use AP scores for placement purposes and allow students with high enough scores to skip the freshman requirement in the subject and begin at the sophomore level. The exemption often counts as a full college course credit toward a college degree.

Special Facilities

A good school is not the military and does not try to force students into a mold. It recognizes student individuality and helps all youngsters realize and develop their individual talents. Principals that protest and say, "We can't give every student a special program," are actually refusing to do their jobs properly. They prefer the simplicity of substandard schools, where students march in lockstep and where the administration and faculty need no creativity or originality. That, incidentally, is one of the disadvantages of a school that carries the subject-centered teaching approach to extremes—especially in the early kindergarten-grade school years, where individuality, initiative and creativity are easily crushed and different rates of development among children require a more individualized approach.

Good schools (even subject-centered schools, if they're truly high quality) tailor their programs to the special needs of every student— the gifted, the handicapped, high-risk youngsters and those with special talents.

Gifted Students

Every quality school encourages gifted students at every grade level to move ahead at their own pace and to do independent study—yes, even kindergarten children. When they're very young, students work with partners. When they reach middle school and high school, they gradually learn to work independently. Such independent study allows youngsters to learn by discovery instead of memorization. Usually youngsters pick study topics that interest them most. The wise teacher then leads them along a path of discovery that not only satisfies their original interest but interrelates it to a wide range of other disciplines— science, math, literature, history, the arts and virtually every other element of the core curriculum. Students in independent study not only work closely with one or more teachers in school, they often have contact or even work with specialists outside school who are usually quite pleased to encourage gifted children. Students in independent studies eventually produce papers and talks summarizing their work and giving them an opportunity to improve writing and presentation skills. Above all, they learn the excitement of learning and imparting what they learned to others. Education becomes a joy instead of a chore.

Good middle schools and high schools also give gifted students special examinations that permit them to "test out" of a course and move to more advanced levels, including advanced placement courses and, if possible, even college-level courses at nearby colleges and universities. Instead of holding back gifted kids, such schools encourage them to move ahead academically at whatever pace best suits them. High school students in the Berkeley, California, area, for example, can take up to two courses per quarter for credit toward college degrees at the University of California if their high school principals nominate them for the program. They continue taking courses in other subjects at their high schools for at least four periods a day.

Syracuse University has a similar program in the East, but instead of making high school students come to the upstate New York campus, the university goes to them. It has trained hundreds of high school teachers in schools throughout the East and Midwest to teach six different college-level courses in their schools. Students who participate earn college credits without altering their daily high school routines.

There are hundreds of similar programs sponsored by colleges in Ohio, Maryland, Washington, New York City and elsewhere, and thousands of high schools eagerly participate in these "university-in-the-school" programs to enhance educational opportunities for gifted students.

Obviously, not all students are college bound or academically prepared for such programs, but good public schools also offer comparable programs for gifted students in business and vocational studies. The question to ask the high school principal is whether the school actively participates in such programs and encourages and prepares students to participate. If it doesn't, find out why. At most poor quality schools, insecure faculties often fear contacts with college level or post-high school programs that might expose their own and their school's inadequacies to students and parents.

Even if there are no colleges nearby, teachers at quality schools should willingly work independently with gifted students—on a one-to-one basis if needed. About 100 U.S. and Canadian high schools participate in the International Baccalaureate, an extremely difficult program consisting of six courses for academically gifted students. Students take three of the courses for two years each and the other three for one year each.

Some states, of course, have special public schools for gifted students—magnet schools. Students must go through rigorous admissions procedures, however. Some are somewhat specialized such as New York City's Bronx High School of Science or High School of Music and Art, and others, such as New York City's Stuyvesant High School, offer broad academic programs. North Carolina, with a widely scattered rural population, has set up residential schools for gifted students. The North Carolina School for the Arts is a boarding school for students gifted in music, drama, writing and the visual arts, while the North Carolina School for Science and Mathematics is a boarding school for students gifted in those disciplines.

The point is that states, communities and schools that care about giving their children a good education make provisions for gifted children of every age. At the very least, you should look for such special programs as independent study or "testing out" credits as signs of quality at the schools you're considering for your children.

Handicapped Students

Under federal law, all public schools must have facilities for the physically handicapped. Any school that doesn't is not only violating federal law, it is showing complete contempt for the needs of children in the community, and the wise parent would do well to walk away from such schools. Specifically, the Rehabilitation Act of 1973 and the Education of All Handicapped Children Act of 1975 require all public schools to provide a free and appropriate education to all children, regardless of their handicaps. The laws also require that handicapped children be placed in the "least restrictive environment" and that every school have an "Individualized Education Program" to meet the needs of each handicapped student.

For millions of children, the laws have meant the ability to attend the same schools as children without handicaps and obtain a more normal education in a happier setting. Tens of thousands of others, with more severe physical, mental and emotional handicaps, couple normal classroom attendance with special "pull-out" sessions with specialists who combine academic instruction with physical or psychological therapy.

In addition to the more evident handicaps, there is another category of handicap that falls into the broad category of "learning disability." Indeed, more than 40% of the more than 4 million handicapped children in the United States are learning disabled—1.4 million in all. Despite the large number, no one is quite certain what it means for most children. The U.S. Department of Education says it is a malfunction in one or more of the basic learning processes of "understanding or using (spoken or written) language" and that it can show up in "an imperfect ability to listen, think, speak, read, write, spell or do mathematical calculations."

The important thing to remember is that learning disabilities have nothing to do with mental retardation or impaired hearing or vision. As many as 10% of otherwise normal and often exceptionally bright children suffer from learning disabilities of one form or another during their childhoods. Some learning disabilities are the result of minor brain damage. Untold others are developmental, and millions of children outgrow them.

Some learning disabilities are specific and relatively easy to identify; others are so vague and undefinable they could apply to all of us at one time or another (if we could remember that far back into our childhoods). In many cases, such disabilities show up only in the form of poor academic work despite great effort and obvious ability to do better. One child with learning disabilities may be impulsive and hyperactive, the next might seem depressed and show no motivation. In some children it shows up in misshapen letters or backward lettering or an inability to read, because letters and words appear garbled. Still other learning-disabled children find it difficult to pay attention or follow instructions or recall information. And there are a thousand other types of behavior that are perfectly normal for most children—if they're not prolonged beyond a reasonable length of time.

Good schools with sensitive, properly trained teachers are quick to pick up such prolonged dysfunctions, and they have remedial specialists to deal with them. Good elementary schools have specially trained remedial teachers for reading, writing and math, and they have other specialists to teach children with learning disabilities how to function normally and happily and work around their disabilities. Then, if they outgrow them, fine; if not, that's fine, too. Children with learning disabilities who are taught properly have as high a success ratio in school and later on in adult life as other children, and good schools try to integrate such children into the mainstream of school education as much as possible.

High-risk Students

High-risk students tend to disrupt normal school routines. Often unable to perform well academically, they resort to misbehavior or violence to draw attention to themselves. The result is damage to the academic environment of the entire school and to academic performance of other students.

Obviously, even the most well-meaning school will not be able to cope with every high-risk student. Some need to be segregated in special schools where they cannot disrupt the school routine for the rest of the student community. As a parent evaluating a school, however, you should try to find out in advance the percentage of high-risk students in the school and exactly how the school copes with them—and whether they send uncontrollable high-risk students elsewhere. Ask for a clear-cut explanation of the school's retention policies and exactly what constitutes academic and behavioral grounds for suspension and dismissal.

Students with Special Talents

Some youngsters who are not "gifted" in the broadest sense are indeed gifted in specific limited areas but quite average or even below average in other areas—the gifted clarinetist who cannot pass chemistry or the superb cabinet maker who cannot fathom poetry. Mediocre schools often fail to identify these students or encourage the growth of their talents. Indeed, some incompetent teachers often discourage such youngsters by ordering them to pay less attention to their special interests and concentrate on "more important things."

A skilled faculty, however, recognizes such youngsters and provides individualized programs that permit them to develop and exploit their talents to the fullest without forcing them to struggle in areas where they are certain to fail. Such students usually need a carefully planned curriculum—one that satisfies all graduation and, where appropriate, college admission requirements. In many cases, specialized magnet schools, such as the North Carolina School for the Arts, may be more appropriate, but any good school willingly adapts its own curriculum requirements to meet the needs of these exceptional youngsters.

Summer School

Another special facility available at better quality schools is summer school, where students who did poorly in a course or lack necessary graduation or college credits can make up the work. Summer school can also offer gifted students an opportunity to do independent study. It lets others take such important noncredit courses as driver education and word processing without interfering in the academic program of the normal school year. And some students often go to summer school just for the fun of being with friends and learning things they might not otherwise study—everything from astronomy to cooking to tennis. In other words, a good school also offers a summer term for remedial work and as an experience in the sheer joy of learning free of the pressures of the regular school term.

Off-campus Academic Alliances

Still another mark of a high-quality school is its ties to off-campus educational resources. A school with a faculty that is secure about its professional skills eagerly seeks and encourages guest experts to visit the school to teach, lecture, perform and otherwise supplement and expand normal academic offerings. In addition to the usual visits by the local police and fire chiefs, such schools call on business leaders, scientists, college professors, writers, artists, signers, musicians and a host of other professionals to enrich the school curriculum. Good schools also take students to off-campus sites to learn how businesses and factories function, to visit restored historical sites and museums, to attend performances at concert halls, theaters and opera houses and to visit other places of interest in the community.

The range and frequency of such outside connections is a reflection of the academic quality of a school at any level. Even children in kindergarten need to connect what they learn in school to the realities of the world outside school.

Business and industry at local levels have always sought to cooperate with nearby schools, but, in substandard schools, insecure faculties often reject such contacts as an infringement on their prerogatives. Better-quality schools encourage these contacts. They not only augment student education, they often lead to many summer jobs and even career opportunities. The schools themselves often benefit in the form of much needed contributions of equipment, supplies and other gifts. Indeed, the U.S. Department of Education estimates that American business sponsors more than 60,000 school-support projects. International Business Machines, Apple and other companies have given free microcomputers to hundreds of schools. General Electric has a career development program involving its employees who serve as mentors to students in science and mathematics studies at many schools near company facilities.

Many colleges, universities and nonprofit organizations also work with schools that seek such cooperation. Scientists at the Lawrence Livermore National Laboratory of the University of California at Berkeley take sixth and seventh graders at a local magnet school on field trips and help them with research projects. In other communities, schools recruit retirees who have had careers in special areas to serve as mentors.

So, in evaluating any school, ask the principal how much the school taps outside resources. It's a measure of how eager the school is to educate its children to the maximum; it's a measure of whether the school administration and faculty have a sense of involvement in a common enterprise with parents and the community to give children the best possible education.

Parents' Organizations

Finally, ask the principal about the parents' organizations and their specific functions, responsibilities and degree of input. Find out how big they are and the percent of parents who participate. Does the school have open house functions and parents' days? How many parents show up? An astonishing 90% of teachers surveyed by the Carnegie Foundation for the Advancement of Teaching cited lack of parental support as a major problem in their schools. So ask whether parent apathy is a problem at each school you visit. If less than 50% of parents participate in the parents' organization, you're dealing with a school where parents may not have high educational goals for their children—and that may be reflected in the quality of education offered and the peer pressures your children will feel.

It's important at every school for parents to be in constant contact with teachers and student advisors to share concerns and discuss the failures and triumphs of the children—to act as a team to help children succeed. Each has a different role in educating youngsters, but it's important that they coordinate their efforts and reinforce each other's expectations for students. Good schools hold parent-teacher conferences at least once every semester.

Ask the principal for names of parents to contact to find out more about parent organizations and use that opportunity to get the views of parents with children in school about educational quality. Ask them what they think about the school atmosphere. Is it friendly, warm, exciting, boring, intimidating? Do they think the school is meeting the needs of their children? Do they feel they have adequate access to the principal and the faculty?

Remember, however, that parents are usually not professional educators and are probably not qualified to evaluate education. Most have their own particular beliefs and prejudices. So try instead, if you speak with parents, to get an idea of the general atmosphere and student morale at school rather than views on theories of education.

Unfortunately, you may find that there is a relatively inactive and perhaps even nonexistent parent organization at some high schools (other than sports booster clubs). Many parents feel the high school years are the time to let go of their children and let them become independent and fend for themselves. Actually, many teenagers need more guidance than when they were infants learning to walk. The dangers facing school youngsters today are everywhere—drugs, alcohol, crime, teenage pregnancy—as are the possibilities of decisions that can close doors to opportunities. Poor curriculum planning and selection of the wrong high school courses can lock children out of the best colleges and universities.

The high school years are not the time for parents to let go, and you'll find that schools with the best education have strong, active parents' organizations that support the academic goals of the principal and faculty and encourage their children to excel academically and participate in school activities.

TEACHER INTERVIEWS

By the time you meet for personal interviews with your children's future teachers, most of your questions about the school will have been answered. There should be little left to ask them except their assessments of the school and its quality of education. Do they send their children there? Would they? Are they aware of the school's educational goals, and can they state them? What are their classes like, and what's it like teaching at the school? Ask them what they consider their major problems. As pointed out before, teachers in substandard schools often spend half their time filling out forms for bloated bureaucracies instead of teaching.

Ask teachers what they consider their worst problems at school. Well over half the public school teachers in the United States list disruptive student behavior, vandalism, drugs and alcohol. Nearly half say student violence against other students is a problem, and about one-quarter say student violence against teachers is a problem. Little learning takes place in schools devastated by these serious problems, and it would be tragic to settle in an area where you're forced to send your children to such schools.

Even if your children are only approaching kindergarten age, it's important to find out if these serious social problems exist anywhere in your school district or in any district to which your children may have to be bused. Besides the problems listed above, ask about theft, gambling, fighting and racial problems and bigotry.

Once again, ask teachers (as tactfully as you can) where they went to college, what degrees they obtained and what their educational qualifications are for teaching the grade or course. Remember especially that teachers in the early elementary years have to be particularly well-versed in a wide range of courses—English, math, history, geography, civics, science, music and art. Less than 30% of elementary school teachers say they're qualified to teach science, and many others cannot teach music or art. Make certain your children's teachers are qualified to teach all these subjects or, if not, whether the school provides specialists to take up the slack on a regular basis. Find out what they know before you enroll your children in their classes. Ask them how long they've been at the school and where else they taught—and why they left their last post. Ask again about the number of classes and hours they teach, whether they have enough preparation time and whether teaching conditions at the school are good. Do they have a teachers' lounge? Are they happy about the pay? Do they like most of the children—and the parents? Ask whether they chose the courses and grades they teach. Ask whether they supervise any extracurricular or athletic activities—and whether they chose to do so or had to as part of their jobs. Ask whether they're forced to assume any menial duties in school—work that demeans them and lowers student esteem for the faculty. The best schools treat faculty with respect and dignity, and that, in turn, seems always to insure student respect and esteem for teachers. And finally, ask teachers what one or two major changes they would make, if they could, in the way things are done at school.

Many of these questions are quite personal, and many teachers and administrators may resent your probing this deeply. But remember that you are entrusting your children's minds and bodies to these people, and you have every right to know everything about them—at least until all schools and teachers adhere to a single set of high standards that all Americans can trust to insure their children a uniformly excellent education. Remember, too, that you're a consumer who will directly or indirectly spend thousands of dollars a year in state and local school taxes for many years before, during and after your children attend school. You have a right to know what your children will get for your money!

A FINAL WORD

Remember as you probe and evaluate each school to look for positives as well as negatives. There is no question that the United States has a shamefully large number of substandard public school systems. Using a standard of one to six, the U.S. Labor Department ranked the reading skills required for various jobs in 1990 and the reading skills of recent U.S. high school graduates. Jobs as scientists, lawyers and engineers required reading skills of six, manual labor only one, and the average nonmilitary job—such as retail sales and skilled construction work—a reading skill of three. The average high school graduate had a reading skill of only 2.6 and was, therefore, unqualified to hold an average job.

So thousands of public schools are failing millions of American children. They don't have to fail yours, however, because there are many that are doing a magnificent job. It's just a question of finding and identifying them. I hope this book will give you the means to find those other, better schools for your children. Good luck.

CHECKLIST
A Visit with the Principal and Teachers
(Report Card Nos. 4–8)

☐ Principal's credentials
☐ Authority

☐ Principal's evaluation of school
___ Academic goals
___ Student achievement
___ Faculty
___ Strengths
___ Weaknesses
___ Main problems
___ Accreditation (and/or curriculum audit)
☐ Curriculum
___ Open or restricted
___ Quality of courses
___ Hours of student classtime per week
___ Homework requirements
___ Core curriculum
    ___ English (reading, writing and rhetoric)
    ___ Math
    ___ Social studies (history, civics and geography)
    ___ Science
    ___ Foreign languages
    ___ Fine arts
    ___ Health education
    ___ Public service and extracurricular activities
☐ Teaching methods
___ Interdisciplinary
___ Team teaching
☐ Honors courses
☐ Advanced Placement courses
☐ Special Facilities
___ Programs for gifted students
    ___ Testing out
    ___ University in the school
___ Programs for the handicapped
    ___ Remedial reading, writing, math
    ___ Learning disabilities
___ High-risk students
___ Summer school
___ In-school programs by visiting experts and artists
___ Off-campus academic alliances
☐ Parent-teacher conferences
☐ Parents' organizations
☐ Teacher interviews

PART II

REPORT CARDS FOR YOUR CHILDREN'S SCHOOLS

CHAPTER 6
GRADING THE SCHOOLS

Evaluation of a school and school district is not difficult if you know the right things to look for and the right questions to ask. As the statistics in Part I show, there are too many average and substandard schools in the United States, but there are also many thousands of superior schools. Superficially, most of them—especially the newer ones—look alike. So don't be fooled by appearances. Probe, probe and probe again. If school officials or teachers resent your "nosing around" or have no time to answer your questions, leave—and look for another school!

Superior schools appreciate parental concern for the educational welfare of their children. They recognize parents' rights to know exactly who is going to teach their children, what will be taught and how it will be taught. These are your fundamental rights—and your children's rights.

In the following pages, you'll find a series of Report Cards to help you grade public and private schools, public school districts, principals, faculty, school superintendents and school boards. The Report Cards are straightforward and, for the most part, self-explanatory, although each is preceded by a set of directions. Although many questions in the Report Cards can be answered objectively (for example, average college entrance examination scores), many others call for your own subjective judgments. At times these may differ with judgments of teachers, principals or other parents. After all, the classroom one person considers immaculate may be considered messy by someone else, and the rest room some call clean may be filthy to others. And that's all right. If you think the school bathrooms are filthy, then they are— no matter what anyone else thinks. *Your children* are going to attend that school, and you must be satisfied that it's the right school for them. So don't be afraid to be subjective.

The grading system is the same as in Table 2, Chapter 2, the Comparative Report Card on State Education. Mark "A" for above average, "S" for satisfactory and "F" for inferior, with pluses or minuses to show gradations for each ranking. An item earns an "S" (satisfactory) if it falls within 10% of the national average. It earns an "A" (above average) if it's 10% better than the national average and an "F" (inferior) if it's 10% worse. Add a plus or minus to the grade if the difference from the national average is 15% or more.

Some Report Cards, such as No. 1, School District, ask you to enter a grade in each column; others only require a check mark under the A, S or F columns opposite each question, as in Report Card No. 2, School Profile. In both cases, the Final Grade is figured the same way. Add the number of each of the rankings and put the results opposite "TOTALS" at the bottom. In Figure 2, for example, the totals come to 8 A's, 3 S's, and 1 F for Lake Forest High School's profile (Figure 1 in Chapter 2).

Now balance the "above average" rankings against the "inferiors." In this case, the difference is a balance of 7 A's (A's − 1F = 7 A's). Again, the 10% rule applies. If the balance of A's is more than 10% greater than S's, give the category a final grade of A. The same thing for F's. Lake Forest's profile earns an easy Final Grade of A, because the 7 A's are clearly more than 10% above the total S's (in other words, well above satisfactory). In fact, it's so overwhelmingly above average, it got an A+. Had A's and F's balanced out evenly, the profile would have been graded S for satisfactory. And had there been more F's than A's, the Final Grade would have been F.

Report Cards No. 1 and 2 are especially useful for quick, preliminary evaluations of schools and school districts, because you can get all the data you need for them by mail or telephone and, in the case of clearly substandard schools, avoid long visits needed for in-depth evaluations.

Before visiting any school, fill in as much of every Report Card as you can with data from the school's printed materials and the school superintendent's office. You can then fill in the remaining blanks as you visit the school and interview the principal and faculty. Before doing any grading, though, it may be helpful to make copies of the blank report cards—one set for each school you evaluate.

When doing in-depth evaluations, don't feel you have to answer every question to get an accurate assessment. Indeed, you may find as many as 10% of the questions unanswerable because they are not applicable, as in items E and G in the Lake Forest school profile evaluation in Figure 2. In Item F, it's immaterial how many graduates go to two-year colleges if 86% go to four-year colleges. The percent that go to two-year colleges will obviously be below the national average, but giving the item an F would clearly distort the true picture of the school, whose students are so superior they almost all go to four-year colleges.

Use your judgment about pressing for answers to questions that may be inappropriate for certain age groups or settings. Most questions, however, are those all schools have to answer to earn accreditation by

Figure 2

Report Card No. 2 can give you a quick, preliminary appraisal of high school quality—as in this evaluation of Lake Forest High School, an outstanding Illinois public school, whose profile is in Figure 1 in Chapter 2. The grading system uses "S" for satisfactory (within 10% of the national average); "A" for above average (at least 10% better than the national average); and "F" for inferior (at least 10% worse than national average). Pluses and minuses indicate variations from the three basic grades.

REPORT CARD NO. 2

School Profile

	A	S	F
A. Size*			✓
B. Accreditation (mark F for no, S for yes)		✓	
C. Student-teacher ratio (natl. avg: 17.4) ⑪	✓+		
D Spending per student (natl. avg: $3,739) $8,099	✓+		

For Elementary and Middle Schools Only:

| E. Percent of students functioning at or above grade level (mark A for 85%; S for 65%; F for less) | N.A. | | |

For High School Graduates Only:

F. Percent of graduates enrolling in 4-yr. colleges (natl. avg: 37%) ⟨86%⟩	✓+		
G. Percent of graduates enrolling in 2-yr colleges (natl. avg: 23%) N.A.			
H. Mean verbal SAT score (natl avg: 428) ⟨469⟩		✓	
I. Mean math SAT score (natl. avg: 476) ⟨512⟩		✓	
J. Mean ACT scores			
a. English (natl. avg: 18.5) 21.2	✓		
b. Math (natl. avg: 17.2) 21.9	✓		
c. Social Studies (natl. avg: 17.4) 21.4	✓		
d. Science (natl. avg: 21.4) 24.5	✓		
e. Composite (natl. avg: 18.8) 22.4	✓		
TOTALS	8	3	1

FINAL GRADE ⟨A+⟩

---

*For K–6, mark A for <250, S for 250–500, and F for >500 students. For 7–12, mark A for <500, S for 500–1000, and F for >1000, unless school is divided into houses of 200 students each or less. Then mark A.

regional accreditation associations, and they are questions schools should have to answer to earn accreditation by parents for their children. So try to get as many answers as you can. Remember, too, that almost all the Report Cards are as valid for private and church-related schools as they are for public schools.

Again: Good luck!

Report Card No. 1
School District

DIRECTIONS: This is the shortest but most complex Report Card. Fill it out first, however, because, together with report Card No. 2 (also short, but much simpler), you'll get a quick preliminary evaluation of any school system anywhere. Like anything new, after you've done it once, you'll find it easy—and I promise it will save you lots of wasted time making unnecessary visits to average and substandard schools.

Report Card No. 1 grades school districts and compares them with national and state averages. The national averages are already printed in the column "U.S. Stats," meaning U.S. statistics. For the state columns, you'll find the statistics for each state in Table 1, Chapter 2, and the ratings (A, S or F) in Table 2, Chapter 2. Enter them in the Report Card in the appropriate places.

For the school district, get the statistics from the school superintendent's office, then assign each figure a grade by comparing it first with national statistics and then with state statistics. That will give you two grades for each item, showing whether it's A (above average), S (satisfactory or average) or F (inferior) compared to the national average and A, S, or F compared to the state average. Use only the comparison with the U.S. average for the Final Grade. The comparison with state averages is only of interest in states with superior (A) educational systems. If a district within such a state ranks substantially higher than the state average, it is obviously an outstanding school—and your search may well have come to an end.

Grade Board Quality and Teacher Input on the basis of your interview with the school superintendent or his staff. School Board Agendas is optional. If you can get this information, fine. If not, leave it blank and use the rest of the data to grade the district. Grade agendas A if they are dominated by legitimate school affairs (budgets, quality of education) and F if dominated by antieducation issues (prayer in school, creation science, book banning). If the agendas seem mixed, grade the item S.

	U.S.* Stats	State* Stats Rating	School District Stats Rating vs. U.S.	Rating vs. State	Final Rating
A. Spending per pupil	$3,739	___	___	___	___
B. Spending on schools as % of all govt. spending	24.2%	___	___	___	___
C. Teacher salaries	$28,044	___	___	___	___
D. Student-teacher ratio	17.4	___	___	___	___
E. Grad/dropout rates	72.6%/ 27.4%	___	___	___	___
F. Student behavior problems (as reported by supt.)					___
G. Teacher input/authority (from Report Card 4)		NOT APPLICABLE FILL IN FINAL GRADES ONLY			___
H. School board quality (from Report Card 3)					___
I. School board agendas					___
J. Accreditation (mark A for yes, F for no, S for no with good reasons)					___
TOTALS					___

FINAL GRADE _____

*From Tables 1 and 2, Chapter 2

Report Card No. 2
School Profile

DIRECTIONS: Put a check mark under "A" (above average) if the school statistic is 10% or more above the national average listed in parentheses and "F" (inferior) if it is 10% or more below the national average. If the item falls within 10% of the national average, grade it "S." Use plus or minus gradations where appropriate. Total the A's, S's, and F's at the bottom of each column, then balance the A's against the F's. If the difference shows either to be within 10% of the total S's, give the category a final grade of S (satisfactory). If the balance shows either A's or F's to be 10% more than the total S's, grade the category F or A, whichever predominates.

For the first item on size of school, mark A for elementary schools with enrollments of less than 250, S for enrollments of 250 to 500 and F for enrollments of more than 500. For middle and high schools, mark A for enrollments of less than 500, S for enrollments of 500 to 1,000 and F for enrollments above 1000.

	A	S	F
A. Size	___	___	___
B. Accreditation (and/or curriculum audit) (mark F for no, S for yes)	___	___	___
C. Student-teacher ratio (avg: 17.4)	___	___	___
D. Spending per student (natl. avg: $3,739)	___	___	___

For Elementary and Middle Schools Only:

E. Percent of students functioning at or above grade level in . . .

	A	S	F
1. Reading	___	___	___
2. Writing	___	___	___
3. Math	___	___	___
4. Science	___	___	___

(Mark A for 85%; S for 65%; F if less)

For High Schools Only:

	A	S	F
F. Percent of graduates enrolling in 4-yr. colleges (natl. avg: 37%)	___	___	___
G. Percent of graduates enrolling in 2-yr, colleges (natl. avg: 23%)	___	___	___
H. Mean verbal SAT score (natl. avg: 424)	___	___	___
I. Mean math SAT score (natl. avg: 476)	___	___	___
J. Mean ACT scores			
a. English (natl. avg: 18.5)	___	___	___
b. Math (natl. avg: 17.2)	___	___	___
c. Social Studies (natl. avg: 17.4)	___	___	___
d. Science (natl. avg: 21.4)	___	___	___
e. Composite (natl. avg: 18.8)	___	___	___
TOTALS	___	___	___

FINAL GRADE _____

Report Card No. 3
Superintendent and School Board

DIRECTIONS: Opposite each question, simply put a check under each board member's name if the answer is yes. If the answer is no, leave the space blank.

There is one exception—the question on anti-education issues. As indicated, if any board member was elected on a platform of anti-education issues (prayer in school, creation science, book banning), give that board member an automatic F in the TOTALS under his name, no matter what other grades he got.

Do not put a grade opposite current job. Simply list what it is. Then, for the next question, "Does job qualify member for board?", put a check mark if you think the answer is yes. Remember, though, experience not directly related to education can nevertheless qualify a person for board membership. Someone with high-level management or financial experience or experience in other professions might well qualify.

School Board Members
(List names under each number)

	1	2	3	4	5	6	Supt.
College degree (accredited college)	___	___	___	___	___	___	___
Graduate school degree	___	___	___	___	___	___	___
Current job	___	___	___	___	___	___	___
Does job qualify member for board?	___	___	___	___	___	___	___
Experience as educator	___	___	___	___	___	___	___
If elected on anti-education issues mark F here and below opposite "TOTALS"	___	___	___	___	___	___	___
TOTALS	___	___	___	___	___	___	___

FINAL GRADE, QUALITY OF BOARD _____
(Enter here and on Report Card No. 1)

Report Card No. 4
Professional Input and Authority
(Who Runs the Schools?)

DIRECTIONS: Instead of putting checks, put an automatic A opposite each item if the answer is either "Faculty" or "Principal." Put an F opposite items if the answer is "School Board" or "State," and an S for items if the answer is Superintendent. Find the totals for A's, S's and F's and proceed as you did in Report Card No. 2, finding the difference between A's and F's and seeing if the balance is more or less than 10% of the total S's.

Who Determines . . .

	Faculty	Principal	Sup't.	School Bd.	State
Textbooks	_____	_____	____	_____	____
Lesson plans	_____	_____	____	_____	____
Curriculum	_____	_____	____	_____	____
Student promotion and retention	_____	_____	____	_____	____
Standards of student behavior	_____	_____	____	_____	____
Student discipline	_____	_____	____	_____	____
Which courses teachers teach	_____	_____	____	_____	____
Which grades teachers teach	_____	_____	____	_____	____
Teacher evaluation	_____	_____	____	_____	____
Selection of new teachers/principal	_____	_____	____	_____	____
Budget allocation	_____	_____	____	_____	____
TOTALS	_____	_____	____	_____	____

FINAL GRADE, PROFESSIONAL INPUT _____
(Enter here and on Report Card No. 1)

Report Card No. 5
School Policies

DIRECTIONS: Put a check mark under A (above average), S (satisfactory) or F (inferior) for each item, then find the totals for each column. Balance the A's and F's as before and compare the difference to the total S's.

A note about graduation requirements: The graduation requirements listed are the minimum course requirements for admission to many of the 300 most selective U.S. colleges and universities (check *Barron's Profiles of American Colleges*). They are also considered the minimum core curriculum requirements by the U.S. Department of Education and most leading American educators. Schools that match those graduation requirements should be graded A; schools that fall one year short of those requirements should be graded S; and schools falling two years short should be graded F.

	A	S	F
A. Clear academic goals	___	___	___

B. High school graduation
requirements

	A	S	F
1. English (4 yrs.)	___	___	___
2. Mathematics (3 yrs.)	___	___	___
3. Science (3 yrs.)	___	___	___
4. Social studies (3 yrs.)	___	___	___
5. Foreign language (3 yrs.)	___	___	___
6. Fine arts (2 yrs.)	___	___	___
7. Physical education (1 yr.)	___	___	___
8. Health (1 yr.)	___	___	___

C. Open vs. restricted curriculum (Student electives: open—F; closed in 9th & 10th grades—S; closed for all but 8 courses—A)   ___ ___ ___

D. Required core curriculum   ___ ___ ___

E. Homework requirements (S—10 min. per grade level; A—15 min. per grade)   ___ ___ ___

F. Hours of classroom instruction (Avg: 22)   ___ ___ ___

G. Parent-teacher conferences (S—1 per year; A—1 per semester)   ___ ___ ___

H. Rules and regulations
(mark F for lax or cruel; A for strict but fair; S for vague)

	A	S	F
1. Absence	___	___	___
2. Lateness	___	___	___
3. Failure to do homework	___	___	___
4. Minimum grades required for sports participation	___	___	___
5. Cheating	___	___	___
6. Lack of student academic effort	___	___	___
7. Academic failure	___	___	___
8. Incomplete courses	___	___	___

I. Academic policies

	A	S	F
1. For switching courses	___	___	___
2. For switching teachers	___	___	___
3. Tracking			
a. By academic achievement	___	___	___
b. By diploma category (academic, general, vocational)	___	___	___
4. Teaching methods			
a. subject-centered approach vs. student-centered approach	___	___	___
b. Interdisciplinary teaching	___	___	___
c. Team teaching	___	___	___
5. Class scheduling (modules or traditional)	___	___	___

	A	S	F
6. Class interruptions			
a. Announcements	___	___	___
b. Bells	___	___	___
c. Administrative procedures	___	___	___
J. Rules of behavior			
1. Dress code	___	___	___
2. Grooming code	___	___	___
3. Out-of-school behavior code	___	___	___
K. Behavioral discipline			
1. Lying	___	___	___
2. Vandalism	___	___	___
3. Theft	___	___	___
4. Criminal assault	___	___	___
5. Violence against teachers	___	___	___
6. Fighting	___	___	___
7. Disruptive or coercive behavior	___	___	___
8. Drugs: narcotics and alcoholic beverages	___	___	___
9. Dangerous weapons or explosives	___	___	___
10. Tobacco	___	___	___
11. Gambling	___	___	___
12. Physical threats or verbal abuse	___	___	___
13. Skateboards	___	___	___
14. "Walkmans," radios, etc.	___	___	___
15. Violation of dress and grooming codes	___	___	___
16. Violation of off-campus behavior code	___	___	___
L. Corporal punishment	___	___	___
TOTALS	___	___	___

FINAL GRADE _____

Report Card No. 6
School Faculty

DIRECTIONS: Put a check mark under A (above average), S (satisfactory) or F (inferior) for each item, then find the totals for each column. Find the difference between A's and F's, as before, and compare with total S's to see if it exceeds or is within 10% of Average.

	A	S	F
A. Percentage with degrees in subjects they teach	___	___	___
B. Percentage with at least 8 hours of college courses in subjects they teach	___	___	___
C. Rank in college graduating class	___	___	___
D. Percentage with master's degrees	___	___	___

	A	S	F
E. Teacher salaries	___	___	___
F. Reward system for teachers			
1. "Master teacher" classification	___	___	___
2. Special awards	___	___	___
G. Average tenure	___	___	___
H. Turnover rate	___	___	___
I. Absentee rate	___	___	___
J. Classes/day	___	___	___
K. Preparation time/day	___	___	___
L. Faculty lounge	___	___	___
M. Awareness of school academic goals	___	___	___
N. Teacher choice of courses taught	___	___	___
O. Teacher choice of grades taught	___	___	___
P. Teacher choice of sports coached	___	___	___
Q. Teacher choice of extracurricular activities	___	___	___
R. Own classroom	___	___	___
S. Private office	___	___	___
T. Teaching time vs. paperwork time	___	___	___
U. Time for student conferences	___	___	___
V. Menial duties (lunchroom, hallway supervision)	___	___	___
W. Awareness of school goals	___	___	___
X. Major student problems			
1. Disruptive student behavior	___	___	___
2. Violence against students	___	___	___
3. Violence against teachers	___	___	___
4. Alcohol	___	___	___
5. Drugs	___	___	___
6. Student absenteeism	___	___	___
7. Student apathy	___	___	___
8. Lack of parental support	___	___	___
9. Other	___	___	___
Y. Discretion in handling student discipline	___	___	___
Z. Control over student promotion and retention	___	___	___
TOTALS	___	___	___

FINAL GRADE _____

Report Card No. 7
Individual Teacher and Principal Evaluations

DIRECTIONS: On most items, grade each teacher and the principal A (above average), S (satisfactory) or F (inferior) for each item listed in Report Card No. 7.

Five items call for yes or no answers:

B. College degree (accredited)—Mark S for yes and mark F for no or for degrees from unaccredited colleges.

C. Graduate degree (accredited)—For teachers, mark A for yes, S for no. For the principal, mark S for yes, F for no. Mark F for degrees from unaccredited universities.

D. Majored in course taught—Mark A for yes, S for No.

E. Studied at least eight college courses in course taught—Mark S for yes, F for no.

F. Principal still teaches—A for yes, S for no.

	Teacher A	Teacher B	Teacher C	Teacher D	Teacher E	Principal
A. Awareness of school academic goals						
B. College degree (accredited)						
C. Graduate degree (accredited)						
D. Majored in course taught						
E. Studied at least 8 college courses in course taught						
F. Principal still teaches						
G. Sensitivity to and rapport with students						
H. Control of class						
I. Class atmosphere/ student responses						
J. Class activity (busy work, lively discussion, tests?)						
K. Teacher knowledge of material						
L. Asks leading questions (leads instead of lectures)						

	Teacher A	Teacher B	Teacher C	Teacher D	Teacher E	Principal
M. Teaches critical thinking	_____	_____	_____	_____	_____	_____
N. Interdisciplinary teaching	_____	_____	_____	_____	_____	_____
O. Helps students learn by doing, makes them active participants	_____	_____	_____	_____	_____	_____
P. Teacher assessment of school	_____	_____	_____	_____	_____	_____
TOTALS	_____	_____	_____	_____	_____	_____

FINAL GRADE FOR TEACHERS _____

FINAL GRADE FOR PRINCIPAL _____

Report Card No. 8
School Facilities

DIRECTIONS: Grade each item A (above average), S (satisfactory) or F (inferior) and find the totals for each category. This is the longest report card. It is one you'll have to fill out as you tour the school building. There are places for you to mark totals as you tour each facility. You can carry these totals to the bottom of the Report Card to calculate a final grade at the end of the day.

Report Card No. 8
School Facilities

	A	S	F
I. Neighborhood			
A. Cleanliness	_____	_____	_____
B. Income level (high, average, low)	_____	_____	_____
C. Safety	_____	_____	_____
D. Loitering	_____	_____	_____
TOTALS	_____	_____	_____

	A	S	F

II. School Yard & Building

	A	S	F
A. Attractiveness	___	___	___
B. Maintenance	___	___	___
C. Safety	___	___	___
D. Exterior fencing	___	___	___
E. Loitering outside	___	___	___
F. Building exterior	___	___	___
TOTALS	___	___	___

III. School Interiors

	A	S	F
A. Hallways			
1. Physical Appearance			
a. Condition of floors, walls and ceilings	___	___	___
b. Lighting	___	___	___
c. Safety	___	___	___
i. Fire exits	___	___	___
ii. Fire extinguishers	___	___	___
d. Temperature	___	___	___
e. Odors	___	___	___
f. Facilities for handicapped	___	___	___
2. Atmosphere			
a. Noise level			
i. Shouting	___	___	___
ii. Bells	___	___	___
iii. Announcements	___	___	___
iv. Classroom noises	___	___	___
b. Overcrowding	___	___	___
c. Student conduct			
i. Loitering in halls	___	___	___
ii. Facial expressions	___	___	___
iii. Response to strangers	___	___	___
iv. Shoving	___	___	___
v. Fighting	___	___	___
B. Administration Office			
1. Physical appearance			
a. Walls, floors	___	___	___
b. Desks, equipment	___	___	___
c. Availability of materials	___	___	___
2. Atmosphere			
a. Number of students	___	___	___
b. Noise level	___	___	___
c. Staff attitude			
i. Toward students	___	___	___
ii. Toward visitors	___	___	___
iii. On telephone	___	___	___
TOTALS	___	___	___

A   S   F

IV. Classrooms
A. Physical Appearance
   1. Walls, ceilings, floors, windows   ____   ____   ____
   2. Lighting   ____   ____   ____
   3. Size (for number of students)   ____   ____   ____
   4. Sufficiency (are there enough or must some clases
      be held in halls, gym, cafeteria?)   ____   ____   ____
   5. Number of students/teacher   ____   ____   ____
   6. Safety (fire extinguishers)   ____   ____   ____

B. Atmosphere
   1. Noise level   ____   ____   ____
   2. Odors   ____   ____   ____
   3. Student conduct   ____   ____   ____
   4. Student attitude   ____   ____   ____
   5. Student–teacher rapport   ____   ____   ____
   6. Interruptions by bells or loudspeaker announce-
      ments   ____   ____   ____

C. Materials (fill in categories for your children's grades)
   1. Kindergarten
     a. Wall displays of kids' works   ____   ____   ____
     b. Large open spaces   ____   ____   ____
     c. Proper-sized chairs for each child   ____   ____   ____
     d. Proper-sized tables for individual and group
       use   ____   ____   ____
     e. Learning areas
       i. Blocks   ____   ____   ____
       ii. Reading   ____   ____   ____
       iii. Audiovisual   ____   ____   ____
       iv. Math   ____   ____   ____
       v. Art   ____   ____   ____
       vi. Music   ____   ____   ____
       vii. Science   ____   ____   ____
       viii. Computers   ____   ____   ____
     f. In-class library   ____   ____   ____
     g. Coat closet   ____   ____   ____

   2. Grades 1–6 (elementary school—but sometimes
     only 1–4)*
     a. In-class library   ____   ____   ____
     b. Proper-sized movable desks and chairs for
       each child   ____   ____   ____
     c. Displays of student projects   ____   ____   ____
     d. Learning areas or special classrooms
       i. Reading   ____   ____   ____
       ii. Audiovisual   ____   ____   ____
       iii. Math   ____   ____   ____
       iv. History   ____   ____   ____
       v. Geography   ____   ____   ____
       vi. Science   ____   ____   ____
       vii. Music   ____   ____   ____

	A	S	F
viii. Art	___	___	___
ix. Foreign language (4th grade and up)	___	___	___
x. Technology (calculators, computers, word processors)	___	___	___

3. Grades 7–12 (high school)*
   a. Classrooms (number of students, size of desks and chairs) ___ ___ ___
   b. Special materials (maps in geography, history classes, for example) ___ ___ ___
   c. Laboratories
      i. Students/lab bench ___ ___ ___
      ii. Bench equipment ___ ___ ___
      iii. Lab supplies ___ ___ ___
   d. Computer lab (students/unit) ___ ___ ___
   e. Writing center ___ ___ ___
   f. Music rooms
      i. Sound-proofed ___ ___ ___
      ii. Music stands ___ ___ ___
      iii. Piano in tune ___ ___ ___
      iv. Variety of instruments ___ ___ ___
      v. Sheet music library ___ ___ ___
   g. Art Rooms
      i. Number of easels ___ ___ ___
      ii. Variety of media ___ ___ ___
      iii. Amount of supplies ___ ___ ___
      iv. Number of works in progress ___ ___ ___
   h. Textbooks (check age) ___ ___ ___

TOTALS ___ ___ ___

---

*Some communities divide school years into elementary (1st through 4th grades), middle school (5th through 8th or 9th grades), and high school (9th or 10th through 12th grades). Classroom facilities in middle school, however, should not differ substantially from those in high school.

V. Special Academic Facilities

A. Off-campus activities ___ ___ ___

B. Off-campus academic alliances ___ ___ ___

C. On-campus visits by guest experts, performers, etc. ___ ___ ___

D. Programs for the gifted
   1. Honors caurses ___ ___ ___
   2. AP courses ___ ___ ___
   3. Independent study ___ ___ ___
   4. "Testing out" ___ ___ ___
   5. Courses at nearby colleges ___ ___ ___
   6. "University-in-the-school" programs ___ ___ ___

	A	S	F
E. Programs for handicapped	___	___	___
F. Vocational education	___	___	___
G. Business courses	___	___	___
H. Programs for high-risk students	___	___	___
TOTALS	___	___	___

VI. Library (Media Center)

	A	S	F
A. Books			
1. Number	___	___	___
2. Number/student (Avg: 10/student)	___	___	___
3. Age	___	___	___
4. Condition	___	___	___
B. Periodicals			
1. Number of subscriptions	___	___	___
2. Subscriptions/student (Avg: 1/student)	___	___	___
3. Age	___	___	___
4. Condition	___	___	___
C. Stacks for research	___	___	___
D. Microfiche	___	___	___
E. Copying equipment	___	___	___
F. Computer hook-up to other libraries, data banks	___	___	___
G. Number of reading tables and seats per student	___	___	___
H. Student use (visits per day)	___	___	___
I. Atmosphere	___	___	___
J. Staff	___	___	___
1. Trained librarian	___	___	___
2. Trained aides	___	___	___
TOTALS	___	___	___

VII. Recreational Facilities

	A	S	F
A. Playground (K–6)			
1. Amount of equipment	___	___	___
2. Variety of equipment	___	___	___
3. Condition of equipment	___	___	___
4. Safety	___	___	___
5. Adequate open spaces	___	___	___
6. Trained faculty	___	___	___
B. Gymnasium			
1. Amount of equipment	___	___	___
2. Variety of equipment and number of sports	___	___	___
3. Condition of equipment	___	___	___

	A	S	F
4. Condition of floors, walls, ceilings	____	____	____
5. Size for number of students	____	____	____
6. Safety	____	____	____
7. Temperature	____	____	____
C. Athletics (Grades 7–12)			
1. Number of sports (Avg: 6)	____	____	____
a. Varsity			
i. Boys	____	____	____
ii. Girls	____	____	____
b. Junior varsity			
i. Boys	____	____	____
ii. Girls	____	____	____
c. Intramural			
i. Boys	____	____	____
ii. Girls	____	____	____
2. Safety			
a. Outdoor (equipment and fields)	____	____	____
b. Indoor (equipment and gym)	____	____	____
c. Swimming pool	____	____	____
3. Changing rooms			
a. Physical condition	____	____	____
b. Cleanliness	____	____	____
c. Safety	____	____	____
d. Individual lockers	____	____	____
e. Showers	____	____	____
f. Separation by gender	____	____	____
g. Separate facilities for visiting teams	____	____	____
D. Facilities and adaptive gym for handicapped students	____	____	____
E. Sports faculty and staff			
1. Training to teach sport	____	____	____
2. Training in first aid	____	____	____
3. Athletic trainer	____	____	____
4. Medically trained attendant at sports events	____	____	____
TOTALS	____	____	____

VIII. Extracurricular Activities

	A	S	F
A. Number	____	____	____
B. Percent participation (U.S. avg: 47%)	____	____	____
C. Individual activities (Mark A if school has 9 or more)			
1. Newspaper	____	____	____
2. Yearbook	____	____	____
3. Literary publication	____	____	____
4. Student government	____	____	____
5. Drama society	____	____	____

	A	S	F
6. Band			
7. Orchestra			
8. Singing groups			
9. Academic clubs			
10. Chess club			
11. Social service clubs			
12. Cheerleading/pep club			
13. Photography club			
14. Others (list)			

D. Academic competitions
   1. Interscholastic
   2. Intramural

E. Faculty training

TOTALS

IX. Administrative Services

A. Cafeteria
   1. Atmosphere
   2. Cleanliness
   3. Quality of food

B. Nurse's office
   1. Training
   2. Size
   3. Cleanliness
   4. Supplies

C. Hall locker area
   1. Number (one per student)
   2. Security
   3. Safety

D. Public bathrooms
   1. Number (adequate for girls and boys)
   2. Locations
   3. Security
   4. Cleanliness

E. Guidance Office
   1. Student/counselor ratio
   2. Counselor availability
   3. Counselor specialists
     a. College admissions
     b. Career counseling
     c. Adolescent problems
     d. Sexuality
     e. Substance abuse
     f. Child−parent relations
     g. Psychological counseling

	A	S	F
4. Ties with outside consultants in above fields	___	___	___
5. Guidance library (forms, books and brochures)	___	___	___
F. Bookstore	___	___	___
G. Transportation			
1. Regular school hours	___	___	___
2. After-school hours	___	___	___
H. After-school child care	___	___	___
I. Summer School	___	___	___
TOTALS	___	___	___

X. Parents' Organizations

	A	S	F
A. Number	___	___	___
B. Types	___	___	___
C. Percent parent participation (min. 60%)	___	___	___
D. Responsibilities	___	___	___
E. Input	___	___	___
TOTALS	___	___	___

SUMMARY OF TOTALS:

		A	S	F
I.	Neighborhood	___	___	___
II.	School yard & building	___	___	___
III.	School interiors	___	___	___
IV.	Classrooms	___	___	___
V.	Special academic facilities	___	___	___
VI.	Library	___	___	___
VII.	Recreational facilities	___	___	___
VIII.	Extracurricular activities	___	___	___
IX.	Administrative services	___	___	___
X.	Parents' organizations	___	___	___

GRAND TOTALS ___ ___ ___

FINAL GRADE, SCHOOL FACILITIES _____

Final Report Card
(Enter Final Grades from each Report Card)

State (from Table 2, Chapter 2) ___

Report Card No. 1, School District ___

Report Card No. 2, School Profile ___

Report Card No. 3, Superintendent and School Board ——

Report Card No. 4, Professional Input and Authority ——

Report Card No. 5, School Policies ——

Report Card No. 6, School Faculty ——

Report Card No. 7, Teacher Evaluations ——

Principal Evaluation ——

Report Card No. 8, School Facilities ——

FINAL GRADE ————————

PART III
THE ACADEMIC CURRICULUM

CHAPTER 7

ELEMENTARY SCHOOL— THE EARLY YEARS (KINDERGARTEN THROUGH GRADE THREE)

The cornerstones of education and of every good school curriculum are reading and writing. Children whose schools fail to teach them to read and write well will never recover from that failure. Those who succeed will forever find education a joy and an open road to opportunity and success.

To teach reading and writing effectively, elementary schools must use imaginative, exciting, challenging literature. Too many elementary school teachers, from kindergarten through third grade, rely heavily on "basal" readers—and "Dick, Jane and Spot" books that have made learning to read so dull for so long.

There's no question that every child must learn to "see Spot run," but they'll learn to do so far better if Spot would also wiggle, jump, stomp and fly like Snoopy. In other words, there's no reason reading at any level should be dull, and many successful elementary school reading programs have reduced their reliance on, and even done away with, basal readers and workbooks. Quite simply, they're boring. They take the fun out of learning and are often counterproductive. Every parent who has put up with a child's incessant "why's?" knows that children have a deep desire to learn. Unfortunately, slavish reliance on basal readers instead of good children's literature can easily destroy that desire. So, as you evaluate elementary schools, find out how the curriculum is taught as well as what is taught. Be certain that most reading time is spent with classic children's literature instead of basal readers. (See Table 3 for a list of good children's literature for kindergarten through third grade.)

In addition to basal readers, many substandard schools rely heavily on worksheets and workbooks for teaching math, science and social studies. One-third of all kindergarten teachers use such worksheets and workbooks, which, like basal readers, are designed to make teaching easy—and learning dull. Top educators agree that most five-year-olds lack the attention span (and manual dexterity) to sit for long periods doing repetitive paper-and-pencil exercises with numbers and letters. So, again, find out how the curriculum is taught as well as what is taught. Children are as eager to learn math, science and history as they are to learn to read and write, but they must be taught by allowing them to manipulate objects that turn learning into fun.

Blocks, counting rods and number games make learning mathematics fun; a play kitchen makes learning science and measurements fun while also teaching children to cooperate and share. In other words, the kindergarten curriculum must not only cover the basic elements of the core curriculum, it must do so in a way that makes a child's first experience with learning in school a happy, exciting adventure. Kindergarten can teach children to look forward to the beginning of each school year with either eagerness or dread. It's up to you as a parent to select your children's kindergarten carefully and wisely.

The curriculum below for kindergarten and the rest of elementary school is presented by subject (English, math, science) as in middle school and high school. Unlike high school, where a different teacher has a fixed number of periods each week for each subject, one teacher usually teaches all subjects in the early years of elementary school. An elementary school teacher, therefore, obviously needs a broad base of knowledge in all core curriculum subjects, and it's important to find out if that is indeed the case before enrolling your children in any elementary school. Less than one-fourth of all elementary school teachers consider themselves qualified to teach science, according to the National Survey of Science and Mathematics. A teacher who is unqualified to teach a subject—science, music, art or any other subject—and a school that fails to provide specialists to do the job well deprive your children of basic elements of their education at the most critical time in their educational lives.

Figure 3 outlines a broad, "minimum" curriculum worked out by the U.S. Department of Education for the early years of elementary school. Do not enroll your children in a school whose curriculum does not meet those minimum standards.

Unlike a middle school or high school curriculum, the kindergarten through third grade curriculum is more flexible in terms of the hours devoted to each core curriculum subject. Also, the lines between subjects are not clearly defined—especially in the early grades, when teacher-directed story-reading might at one and the same time improve children's vocabularies and reading abilities while teaching history or science.

Figure 3

Outline of a minimum acceptable curriculum for kindergarten through 3rd grade in an "average" elementary school.

Subject	Kindergarten through Grade 3
English	Introduction to Reading and Writing (phonics, silent and oral reading, basic rules of grammar and spelling, vocabulary, writing and penmanship, elementary composition and library skills)
Social Studies	Introduction to History, Geography and Civics (significant Americans; explorers; native Americans; American holidays, customs and symbols; citizenship; and landscape, climate and mapwork)
Mathematics	Introduction to Mathematics (numbers; basic operations; fractions and decimals; rounding; geometric shapes; measurement of length, area and volume; bar graphs; and estimation and elementary statistics)
Science	Introduction to Science (plants and animals, the food chain, the solar system, rocks and minerals, weather, magnets, energy and motion, properties of matter and simple experiments)
Foreign Language	[Optional]
Fine Arts	Music and Visual Art (songs, recordings, musical sounds and instruments, painting, craftmaking and visual effects)
Physical Education/ Health	Physical Education and Health (body control; fitness; sports, games and exercises; sportsmanship; safety; hygiene; nutrition; and drug prevention education)

Source: *James Madison Elementary School, A Curriculum for American Students,* William J. Bennett, Secretary, U.S. Department of Education.

It's important that kindergarten children attend full-day rather than half-day programs. Full-day programs should run at least four days a week and preferably five. There should be considerable parental involvement, especially on field trips, which should be scheduled at least once every two weeks.

As in first, second and third grades, teachers in kindergarten must touch all areas of the core curriculum—English, math, social studies, science, art, music, foreign languages, health, physical education and public service. They can do much of this by reading aloud stories that combine many topics. Teacher-directed storytime should take up a significant part of each day. Five-year-olds may not be able to differentiate between a fairy tale and a story from history or science, but, if such tales are well written and read aloud, they impart knowledge of fiction, poetry, history, science and even foreign languages.

Kindergarten is a time for social development, and one of the teacher's most important tasks is to teach the children to work and share with other children. Calm, clear explanations of moral behavior—"what we do" and "what we don't do"—is an essential element of the kindergarten curriculum. The teacher must insist on order and firm, quiet, fair discipline. This is also a time for development of work habits, and, again, the teacher must teach these.

Flexibility is another characteristic to look for in kindergarten programs and teaching methods. Every child develops at different rates at different ages, and the minimum "achievement" levels for kindergarten may prove too much for some five-year-olds and far too simple for others. Some children will be able to read well when they finish kindergarten; others will not. Children who are able to read when they finish kindergarten have a slight advantage when they begin first grade, but by the middle of the year, almost all the other children will have caught up. So don't put too much stock in achievement tests that measure a child's "academic" progress at the end of kindergarten. The results will probably be meaningless within six months.

By the end of first grade, however, it's essential that all children have mastered reading and writing, although they'll need to rely heavily on phonics to sound out new words, and teacher-led (and parent-led) classroom story reading will still provide their major reading opportunities in school and at home. By second grade, students should be able to handle most reading independently (and silently) at home, without the need to rely on phonics to sound out most words.

Grade three is the last year for students to master all the education "basics"—reading, writing, arithmetic and rhetoric. At the end of third grade, every child should be able to read complex children's literature—every book on the reading list in Table 3 and the front page of any daily newspaper. At that stage, children should also be able to speak and write clearly and distinctly in complete, grammatically correct sentences, free of slang. They should be able to find any information or book in a library, have a complete mastery of addition, subtraction, multiplication and division and know how to work with fractions, decimals and geometric shapes. They should have a rudimentary knowledge of American history and geography, along with a rudimentary knowledge of biology, geology, astronomy, physics, music and art. In other words, they should clearly be quite well grounded in a broad range of subjects.

If a school has failed its children by the end of third grade, it has doomed them to sub-standard performance for the rest of their academic lives. So, before enrolling your children in elementary school, even if they're only entering kindergarten and you're convinced it's a good kindergarten, visit a third grade classroom to be certain the school is achieving the broader, long-range educational goals outlined in Figure 3.

The detailed curriculum below is presented in checklist form for you to use in evaluating any school—public, private or church-related. It combines the best elements of the Department of Education curriculum with curricula from a number of the finest U.S. public and private schools. To see if the school's curriculum is up to standard, discuss each element with the teacher of the particular grade or course. For example, let's say you're evaluating a kindergarten. In talking with the prospective teacher, ask about the specific elements from the curriculum described below. Ask whether children learn "complete familiarity with the alphabet" and whether they learn "to recite, read and write it with ease and match capital and small letters." If so, put an "S" (satisfactory) on the line in the margin next to "Preparation for Reading and Writing" in the kindergarten English curriculum. Do the same with every other element of the kindergarten curriculum and the curriculum of any other grade you think you should evaluate in the school. If the school's curriculum is below standard (if, for example, it waits until third grade to cover material listed below as second grade work), put an "F" (inferior) in the margin. If the curriculum is well above standard, put an "A" (above average) in the margin. As you did with the Report Cards in Part II, compare the number of A's, S's and F's to develop a final grade for the school's curriculum.

Keep in mind, as you read through the curriculum for each grade, that it details what a child should know at the *end* of each year—not on the first day! So some of the concepts in the kindergarten may seem quite advanced for a child beginning kindergarten—especially as you look at your own five-year-old in the summer before kindergarten. But the concepts listed for kindergarten children are those they should learn during the school year and master by the time they are six and ready for first grade. Similarly, the concepts listed in the first grade curriculum are those children should have mastered by the time they enter second grade.

Kindergarten Curriculum
English

1. *Preparation for reading and writing.* Complete familiarity with the alphabet, including ability to recite, read and write it with ease and match capital and small letters. _____
2. *Elementary phonics.* Letter-sound associations. Sounding out and naming letters at beginning of three-letter and four-letter words. Reading and rhyming short words, such as man and ran. _____
3. *Teacher-directed storytime* takes up significant part of day. Children have read-along copies of many stories and poems and are encouraged to read aloud, according to abilities. Cross-disciplinary stories introduce children to subjects like history, science. Difference between real and make-believe is also taught—for example, that elephants such as Babar do not really talk or wear clothes. _____
4. *Writing.* Students dictate their own words and stories to teacher who slowly transcribes words on the chalkboard. (Teacher transcriptions of children's words into written words are a key element in learning at this age, and this is a critical teaching technique for every kindergarten.) Some children learn to write short words—spelled phonetically, correctly or incorrectly (immaterial at this age). All learn to write their own first and last names correctly. _____

Table 3

Suggested readings from classic children's literature for students in kindergarten through third grade. The list was compiled by the U.S. Department of Education for its classic report, *James Madison Elementary School, A Curriculum for American Students,* by then–Secretary of Education, William J. Bennett.

Readings for kindergarten through grade 3

Behind the Back of the Mountain: Black Folktales from Southern Africa, Verna Aardema
Aesop for Children, Aesop
Hans Christian Andersen's Fairy Tales, Hans Christian Andersen
Anno's Alphabet and *Anno's Counting House,* Mitsumasa Anno
Wiley and the Hairy Man, Molly Bang
Once in Puerto Rico, Pura Belpre

Madeline books, Ludwig Bemelmans
The Three Billy Goats Gruff, Susan Blair
Freddy the Detective, Walter R. Brooks
The Pied Piper of Hamelin, Robert Browning
The Story of Babar, the Little Elephant, Jean de Brunhoff
Mike Mulligan and His Steam Shovel and *The Little House,* Virginia Lee Burton

The Very Hungry Caterpillar, Eric Carle
Jack and the Three Sillies, Richard Chase
The Ramona and Henry Huggins books, Beverly Cleary
Adventures of Pinocchio, Carlo Collodi
Chanticleer and the Fox, Barbara Cooney
The Courage of Sarah Noble, Alice Dalgliesh
Book of Nursery and Mother Goose Rhymes, Marguerite De Angeli
Drummer Hoff, Barbara Emberley
Ask Mister Bear, Marjorie Flack
The Whipping Boy, Sid Fleischman
Millions of Cats, Wanda Gag
The Three Bears, retold by Paul Galdone
Stone Fox, John Reynolds Gardiner
Grimm's Fairy Tales, Jacob and Wilhelm Grimm
The Wonder Book, Nathaniel Hawthorne
One Fine Day, Nonny Hogrogrian
Little Red Riding Hood, retold by Trina Schart Hyman
John Henry: An American Legend and *The Snowy Day*, Ezra Jack Keats
Pecos Bill, Steven Kellogg
Just So Stories, Rudyard Kipling
The Arabian Nights and *Aladdin and the Wonderful Lamp*, Andrew Lang
Piping Down the Valley Wild, Nancy Larrick
The Story of Ferdinand, Munro Leaf
Pippi Longstocking books, Astrid Lindgren
Swimmy, Leo Lionni
Frog and Toad Together, Arnold Lobel
Mrs. Piggle-Wiggle, Betty MacDonald
Make Way for Ducklings and *Blueberries for Sal*, Robert McCloskey
Every Time I Climb a Tree, poems by David McCord

Anansi the Spider: A Tale from the Ashanti, retold by Gerald McDermott
When We Were Very Young and *Winnie-the-Pooh*, A. A. Milne
Amelia Bedelia, Peggy Parish
Cinderella, Charles Perrault
The Tale of Peter Rabbit, Beatrix Potter
Ride a Purple Pelican and *Read Aloud Rhymes for the Very Young*, Jack Prelutsky
Clementine and *She Be Comin' 'Round the Mountain*, Robert Quackenbush
Curious George books, H. A. Rey
The Dancing Stars: An Iroquois Legend, Anne Rockwell
Where the Wild Things Are and *Chicken Soup with Rice*, Maurice Sendak
The Cat in the Hat, Green Eggs and Ham, Horton Hatches the Egg, and others by Dr. Seuss
Caps for Sale, Esphyr Slobodkina
Noah's Ark, Peter Spier
Abel's Island and *Sylvester and the Magic Pebble*, William Steig
A Child's Garden of Verses, Robert Louis Stevenson
East O' the Sun and West O' the Moon, Gudrun Thorne-Thomsen
Brian Wildsmith's Illustrated Bible Stories, Philip Turner
Alexander and the Terrible, Horrible, No Good, Very Bad Day, Judith Viorst
Ira Sleeps Over, Bernard Waber
Charlotte's Web and *Stuart Little*, E. B. White
Little House books, Laura Ingalls Wilder
The Velveteen Rabbit, Margery Williams
Crow Boy, Taro Yashima
Owl Moon and *The Seeing Stick*, Jane Yolen
Rumpelstiltskin, retold by Paul O. Zelinsky

5. *Library.* Regular visits to school (or town) library to learn layout, rules and how to care for books. _____

6. *Rhetoric* (speaking and listening). Emphasis on speaking grammatically correct English free of slang and such phrases as "ain't," "I don't got none" and "me and Johnny went to the store." Listening courteously, taking turns speaking and raising hands for attention. _____

Mathematics

1. *Preparation for math.* Use of woodblocks and other manipulatives, sorting objects by size, color, shape and other details. _____
2. *Counting.* From one to twenty, forwards and backwards. Should be able to pick up a count at any number—from six, for example, as well as from one—and continue to twenty. _____
3. *Meaning of numbers.* Knowing that the written or spoken numeral three is the same as three blocks or three marbles. _____
4. *Measurement.* Comparative concepts (more than, less than, larger than, smaller than, greater than), building number sense and vocabulary. _____
5. *Simple addition and subtraction* of five and under with each other. Solving story problems with numbers. _____
6. *Time.* Telling the hour, half-hour and quarter-hour on analog clocks. Learning dates of birthdays. _____

Social Studies

1. *History.* Major holidays and the people or events they celebrate. _____
2. *Geography.* The relationship of home and school and the "geography" of the neighborhood—addresses and routes, distances and directions to and from different places. Names of the town, state and country and their relative positions on detailed national and global maps. Concept of other people, both like us and different, living elsewhere on the globe. First exposure to concept of foreign languages. _____
3. *Civics.* Preparation for civics and citizenship education, with explanation of school rules and importance to each child's security and happiness. Importance and value of hard work, honesty, obedience of school rules and playing fairly with others. _____
4. *Field Trips.* All aspects of social studies reinforced with frequent field trips. _____

Science

1. *Biology.* Identification of familiar, everyday plants, animals, parts of the body, sense organs and functions. Learning tied to stories during reading time and to art. _____
2. *Geology.* Identification of simplest topographical features—mountains, valleys, oceans, rivers—and the differences be-

tween a lake and an ocean, a river and a brook or creek. Teaching tied to stories and to math concepts of measurement and comparison. _____

3. *Astronomy.* Extension of geography lessons showing earth in relationship to moon and sun and differences between day and night (with tie-in to learning about time). _____

4. *Physics.* Weather (heat, cold), light, darkness and shadows. Common colors. Ties of physical phenomena to feelings and senses and to art and literature. (Teacher: "It was snowing. How did he feel?" Children: "Cold.") _____

5. *Field trips.* Each of the above reinforced by frequent field trips. _____

Fine Arts

1. *Music.* A half-hour (minimum) of singing a day—alphabet songs, nursery rhymes, folktales. (If the kindergarten teacher cannot play the piano, a good school should provide a music specialist who can. Every kindergarten should at least have a record player.) Tapping and clapping to rhythms. Opportunity to play simple rhythm instruments to accompany singing. _____

2. *Dance and drama.* Part of music and reading programs. Connections between rhythmic tapping, clapping and dance. Children dramatize stories of their own and those read aloud by teacher. _____

3. *Art.* Encouragement of imagination and self-expression; mixing two colors to get a third; experiments with textures, line and geometric shapes. Connections between art and math. A good school offers a wide variety of media for children to manipulate—paints of all kinds, felt pens, clay, papier-mache and wood. _____

Social Development

Rules. Explanation of "what we do" and "what we don't do" in relations with other children, the teacher, parents. Safety reasons for obeying rules. _____

First Grade Curriculum
English

1. *Reading.* Student-led story reading; others intermittently read aloud in unison or follow along silently. Stories, poetry, fairy

tales and legends are used to build vocabularies. Phonics used extensively to teach relationships between letters and sounds. Emphasis on pronunciation, vocabulary building and comprehension (inferring meaning from what is read). _____

2. *Grammar.* Nouns (name words) and verbs (action words) and their agreement; simple sentence structure and basic rules of punctuation (capital lettering, commas, periods). _____

3. *Writing.* Emphasis on alphabet, upper and lower case lettering, handwriting (penmanship), spelling and syllables. Grammar lessons reinforced with short writing assignments (sentences, story summaries, creative works and descriptive "word pictures"). _____

4. *Rhetoric.* Emphasis on pronunciation and enunciation as students read aloud to class. Responding to questions in complete sentences. Listening courteously and attentively as a means of learning and responding intelligently to questions. _____

5. *Library.* Regular visits to borrow books for independent reading. _____

Mathematics

1. *Numeration.* Counting forward and backward from 1 to 100, skip counting by twos, fives, and tens, and instant identification of numbers before and after any number from 1 to 100. The concept of place values (42—the two is in the one's place in the number 42, and the four is in the ten's place). _____

2. *Calculation.* Simple addition and subtraction of all single-digit numbers and double-digit numbers that do not need regrouping ($12 + 12$, for example). Recognition of inverse relationship between addition and subtraction, the meaning of the equals ($=$) sign and the concept of fractions (one-half, one-quarter) as parts of a whole. Recognition that learning numbers is helpful in solving problems in daily life. Simple word problems, using numbers at least up to 10. _____

3. *Geometry.* Recognition of all single-dimension geometric shapes in any position. Concepts of vertical, horizontal and diagonal. _____

4. *Measurement.* Measurement of money, time, capacity, weight and temperature. Concept of estimating, using comparative concepts (later than, heavier than, longer than, hotter than). Construction and use of simple bar graphs. _____

Social Studies

1. *History.* Using the family as basis of instruction, students learn about daily life in various periods of American history and how customs and life in the United States differ from daily life in one or more foreign countries. Superficial exposure to languages of those countries with basic phrases such as "bon jour" and "au revoir" and simple folk songs such as "Frere Jacques." The study of symbols—the flag, Liberty Bell, Uncle Sam—and folklore, legends and patriotic songs. Field trips to restored colonial or frontier villages and ghost towns. _____
2. *Geography.* Basic world geography—the continents, oceans—and study of relief maps showing broad landforms. Connections between landscape, climate, land use, transportation and commerce. _____
3. *Civics.* Stories of moral problems and their solutions. Rotating student assignments for classroom and equipment care and maintenance to teach individual responsibility to the community. Origins and meanings of the Constitution and Bill of Rights. _____

Science

1. *Biology.* Study of growing plants; experiments showing how variations in water, soil and sunlight affect growth. Students predict results, then test their hypotheses, monitoring progress of each experiment and recording the results. _____
2. *Zoology.* The study of animal characteristics and habitats; pet care. _____
3. *Astronomy, meteorology.* The solar system; differences between and causes of day and night. Study of weather conditions and causes. _____
4. *Physics.* Properties of water and air; forms and sources of energy. _____
5. *Field trips* to zoos, botanical gardens, weather laboratories. _____

Fine Arts

1. *Music.* Basic music theory, the staff, notations (tie-in to fractions: half-notes, quarter-notes), rhythms, pitch, volume and timbre. Composition of simple melodies. Access to most percussion instruments. Lessons on other instruments also begin. Daily group singing continues, accompa-

nied by student playing of percussion instruments. Field trips to concerts and recitals. _____

2. *Art.* Emphasis on self-expression, using basic skills instead of undisciplined finger painting. Incorporation of shapes—circles, squares, triangles—in drawings to reinforce geometry lessons about shapes and forms. Drawings of humans progress from kindergarten stick figures to more full-bodied, better-proportioned representations. Field trips to museums. _____

3. *Drama.* Preparation of dramatic presentation—preferably a play written by the class. Field trip to a play or presentation of a play in school by touring professionals specializing in performances for school children. _____

SECOND GRADE CURRICULUM
English

1. *Reading.* More independent reading at home and at least 20 minutes of homework nightly. Strong readers proceed at their own pace. (It's important for second grade teachers to see that all students reach a level of minimum competence in reading, without need for phonics to sound out any but the most complex three-syllable words.) In class, group reading takes up less time and emphasizes comprehension of story structure (plot), character and character motivation. Interpretive skills are developed with recognition that stories have meanings that go beyond plot. Major emphasis on vocabulary building and spelling in conjunction with classroom reading and rote learning of lists. Study of synonyms, antonyms and homonyms, vowels and consonants. _____

2. *Writing.* Cursive writing (script) and increased output of stories, poems, letters and simple book reports. At least one writing assignment daily. Extensive penmanship practice. _____

3. *Grammar.* Review of nouns, verbs, simple sentence structure. Instruction in word order, pronouns and their antecedents, adjectives, contractions and possessives. _____

4. *Library.* Identification of books by title and author. Students must borrow and read at least one book a week (book report required). At least one book must be read over Christmas vacation and three over summer vacation. _____

Mathematics

1. *Numeration.* Total mastery of numeration to 1,000—place values to hundreds; "rounding off" to nearest tens and hundreds; reading, writing and ordering all numbers to 1,000; counting by odd and even numbers and by twos, threes, fives and tens to 1,000. _____
2. *Calculation.* Addition and subtraction of single digit numbers horizontally as well as vertically and addition of columns of three single-digit numbers. Regrouping and addition of three two-digit numbers. Subtraction of any two two-digit numbers. Introduction to concept of algebra by solving addition equations with a missing addend $(2+x=5)$ and subtraction problems with missing subtrahend. Multiplication of any two numbers up to five and introduction to complex fractions. Estimation of large-number addition and subtraction problems. _____
3. *Measurement.* Mastery of money, time and calendar. Mastery of ruler and scale to find lengths and weights. Interpretation of graphs. _____
4. *Geometry.* Properties of two- and three-dimensional shapes; classification of plane and solid figures; identification of edges, sides and angles. _____

Social Studies

1. *History.* The life, times and accomplishments of great Americans in every area of U.S. history—politics, science, social reform, technology, education, industry—and their contributions to the building of the U.S. nation. Study of individual students' family histories and customs, beliefs, histories and geographies of ancestors' homelands. _____
2. *Geography.* Cardinal directions, map symbols, physical and cultural differences between urban, suburban and rural areas. Mastery of use of all types of maps, including road maps; study of different forms of transportation. _____
3. *Civics.* Obligations and privileges of U.S. citizenship and importance of free elections and voting. Review of meanings and origins of U.S. Constitution and Bill of Rights. _____

Science

1. *Biology.* Life cycles and seasonal changes in various organisms. Study of maturation of seeds into plants and produc-

tion of new seeds; study of broad classifications of organisms—vertebrates, invertebrates. Field trip to museum of natural history. _____

2. *Astronomy.* The solar system and the effect of the earth's orbit on the seasons and the effect of the moon on the tides. Field trip to planetarium or an evening return to school with parents for view of moon and stars. _____

3. *Physics.* Magnets and magnetism, the forces of motion, simple machines and their inventors. Student construction of simple machines and magnetic compasses for use in various games and exercises. Field trip, either to a museum, nearby college or industrial company, to illustrate simple machines. _____

Fine Arts

1. *Music.* Advanced musical notation; reading and playing from sheet music instruments such as the recorder or xylophone. Identification of names and sounds of orchestral instruments. Individual student instrumental instruction in its second year. Class "musicale" by all student performers. Field trips to concerts and recitals or in-school performances. _____

2. *Art.* Study of geometric elements of objects; and reproduction on paper or with clay. Disciplined approaches to art. Study of craft forms, photography. Study of form, color and texture and visual effects they create. First efforts to identify and describe content in works of art. Field trips to museums and art exhibits. _____

THIRD GRADE CURRICULUM
English

1. *Reading.* Meanings of prefixes, suffixes and roots and their Latin and Greek origins, as well as etymology of simple words. Students should be able to pronounce correctly any word of three syllables (from children's literature) and find its meaning if they don't know it. Reading now a tool for acquiring knowledge as well as entertainment. Introduction to critical study of literature and understanding of such elements as character development, motivation and underlying meanings. Reading consists of full-length juvenile novels, poetry, plays, fables and nonfiction. Vast expansion of vo-

cabularies and comprehension skills, with ability to pronounce and understand almost everything on the front page of the average daily newspaper. Independent reading expands—again, a book or more a week, but with larger books. One additional book assigned for Christmas vacation reading and three additional books assigned for summer reading.   _____

2. *Writing.* Emphasis on spelling and expansion of vocabularies. Class spelling bees. Penmanship. Introduction to formal craft of writing—outlining, drafting, revising and editing, along with advanced compositional skills, such as paragraphing and paragraph design, use of synonyms to avoid repetition and proper word selection to convey exact meanings. At least one paper due every day and one book report or creative piece each week. A minimum of 30 minutes of homework each night and 90 minutes over the weekend; at superior schools, an hour of homework at night, Monday through Thursday, and 90 minutes to two hours over the weekend. Grammar studies include rules for sentence structure (subject and predicate) and adverbs.   _____

3. *Rhetoric.* Choral reading to improve oral skills. At least two oral reports per student each semester to supplement written reports. Emphasis on clear pronunciation and enunciation in complete, grammatically correct sentences, free of slang.   _____

4. *Library.* Emphasis on basic reference and research skills— using card catalogs, dictionaries, encyclopedias, atlases, indexes and other reference materials.   _____

Mathematics

1. *Calculation.* Mastery of multiplication tables through 12, addition and subtraction of four- and five-digit numbers. Multiplication of two- and three-digit numbers by single digit multiplicands and division of two- and three-digit numbers by single-digit divisors. Recognition of inverse relationship between multiplication and division. Numeration into tens and hundreds of thousands, millions and billions. Mastery of fractions and decimals and conversion from one to the other. Mastery of metric system.   _____

2. *Geometry and measurement.* Units of length, area, volume, weight and time, measurement of areas and volumes using squares and cubes. Interpretation of complex bar and picture graphs. Basics of probability.   _____

3. *Technology.* Introduction to use of calculators and computers. _____

Social Studies

1. *History.* Era of exploration, with focus on such major explorers as Marco Polo, Ericson, Vikings, Columbus, Sir Francis Drake, Balboa and early explorers in North and South America. Culture, beliefs and daily life of Native American peoples—what the explorers found here when they landed. The first American-born explorers (Boone, Lewis and Clark) and westward extension of U.S. frontiers. History of community and state where the children attend school. Field trips to tie in with as many areas of history as possible. _____
2. *Geography.* Tracing explorers' paths and refinement of map-reading and globe-reading skills. Identification of latitude, longitude, the equator, continents, oceans, poles and hemispheres. _____
3. *Civics.* A study of the Massachusetts and Virginia settlements—their ideas about religious tolerance and local government and their historic ties to the Constitution and Bill of Rights. A look at the local community, its people and their ethnic diversity, how it compares with other communities and what it "inherited" from the Massachusetts and Virginia settlements. Appropriate field trips. _____

Science

1. *Biology.* Growth stages of animals, the food chain and interdependency of various forms of life. _____
2. *Geology.* Simple rocks and minerals and their origins and uses. Collection, comparison, classification and recording of shapes, sizes, weights and textures of different rock and mineral samples. Field trip with geologist. _____
3. *Physics and chemistry.* Physical and chemical properties of matter—hardness, softness, melting points, boiling points; conversion from gases to liquids to solids and vice versa; gravity; energy. Magnetism, electricity and electric charges. Field trip to museum or appropriate substitute. _____
4. *Astronomy.* The solar system, planets, moons, stars, asteroids, meteoroids, comets and smaller particles, constellations, galaxies, the universe, space and the history of space exploration. Student demonstration of solar system, with light bulb as the sun and the students themselves as planets.

Demonstration of the earth's rotation and how tilt affects climate and light in the northern and southern hemisphere. How sun's reflected light produces predictable changes in the moon's phases and how it produces eclipses. Composition of planets, stars and sun. Field trip to planetarium. _____

Fine Arts

1. *Music.* Mastery of rhythmic and tonal elements of music and musical notation. Ability to play from sheet music a short piece of music on an instrument of choice. Ability to write short compositions using standard notation and to identify the sounds of virtually every orchestral instrument. Recognition of key signatures and all notations on the staff. Group singing of folk songs and easy-to-sing melodies from semiclassical works such as Gilbert and Sullivan operettas. Student performance of "H.M.S. Pinafore" or equivalent. Field trips to concerts, opera, ballet or live performances at school; videotapes. _____
2. *Art.* Emphasis on accurate, representative drawing—with perspective and contrast between light and dark areas. Mastery of such skills as making posters, working with cardboard, pasting and cutting, making collages, making simple costumes from cloth and making various products out of paper, wood and clay. Field trips to art exhibits or museums are essential at this age. _____

CHAPTER 8

ELEMENTARY SCHOOL— THE LATER YEARS (GRADES FOUR THROUGH SIX)

Few elementary school teachers have the training or knowledge to teach the entire curriculum in fourth, fifth or sixth grade, where academic work becomes almost as complex and demanding as in middle school. Superior schools break up the program and let specialists teach each subject—preferably working as a team to interrelate the entire program. Any elementary school that continues to use one teacher for the entire curriculum is all but certainly substandard, and you would be wise to spend an entire day there to see if the curriculum approaches the one outlined below. If it does not, your children will not get the schooling needed to attend a superior middle school or high school when they finish sixth grade. Figure 4 shows the U.S. Department of Education's minimum acceptable curriculum for fourth through sixth grade. Do not send your children to schools that offer less.

Depending on the population and teacher and school resources, some school districts end elementary school after fifth grade or even fourth grade and combine one or both of those grades into middle school with seventh or seventh and eighth grades. Although such combinations may produce a different social mix for your children, there is no reason for details of the curriculum to vary greatly from the one below, except in the foreign language sector, where the costs of audiovisual equipment and tapes might be too much for a particularly small neighborhood elementary school to afford for only a handful of students. In small districts of this type, your children might have to wait until middle school to begin foreign language studies.

Reading and writing continues to be a mainstay of the curriculum in fourth, fifth and sixth grades, and, as before, superior schools will rely more on good literature than basal readers to teach and stimulate their students. Table 4 provides a suggested reading list for fourth, fifth

Figure 4

Outline of a minimum acceptable curriculum for grades four through six in an "average" elementary school.

Subject	Grades 4 through 6
English	Introduction to Critical Reading (children's literature; independent reading and book reports; more advanced grammar, spelling and vocabulary; composition skills)
Social Studies	Grade 4: U.S. History to Civil War Grade 5: U.S. History Since 1865 Grade 6: World History to the Middle Ages
Mathematics	Intermediate Arithmetic and Geometry (number theory; negative numbers, percentages and exponents; line graphs; the Pythagorean theorem; basic probability)
Science	Grade 4: Earth Science and Other Topics Grade 5: Life Science and Other Topics Grade 6: Physical Science and Other Topics
Foreign Language	Introduction to Foreign Language (basic vocabulary, grammar, reading, writing, conversation and cultural material)
Fine Arts	Music and Visual Art (great composers, musical styles and forms, elementary music theory, great painters, interpretation of art and creative projects)
Physical Education/ Health	Physical Education and Health (team and individual sports, first aid, drug prevention education and appropriate sex education)

Source: *James Madison Elementary School, A Curriculum for American Students,* William J. Bennett, Secretary, U.S. Department of Education.

and sixth graders, all of whom should be able to complete the entire list over their three years in this program.

As with the kindergarten through third grade curriculum, ask each teacher whether his or her course will cover every element in the description set forth below. For example, ask the fourth grade math teacher whether the class studies geometry and such aspects as symmetry and congruence; parallel and perpendicular lines; acute, right and obtuse angles; and the characteristics of polygons. Ask to see the textbook used and check that it covers these elements. If not, give that course an "F" (for inferior) in the blank space in the margin next to it. If the course offering matches the description below, give it an "S" (for sat-

Table 4

Suggested readings from classic children's literature for students in grades four through six. The list was compiled by the U.S. Department of Education for its classic report, *James Madison Elementary School, A Curriculum for American Students,* by then-Secretary of Education, William J. Bennett.

Readings for grades 4 through 6.

Born Free, Joy Adamson

Little Women, Louisa May Alcott

Sounder, William H. Armstrong

Tuck Everlasting, Natalie Babbitt

Peter Pan, J. M. Barrie

Crickets and Bullfrogs and Whispers of Thunder: Poems and Pictures, Harry Behn

Stories of the Gods and Heroes, Sally Benson

Sundiata: The Epic of the Lion King, Roland Bertol

The Dog Days of Arthur Cane, T. Ernesto Bethancourt

Doctor Coyote: A Native American Aesop's Fables, retold by John Bierhorst

The Secret Garden, Frances Hodgson Burnett

The Summer of the Swans, Betsy Byars

A New Treasury of Children's Poetry: Old Favorites and New Discoveries, edited by Joanna Cole

Prairie Songs, Pamela Conrad

James and the Giant Peach and *Charlie and the Chocolate Factory,* Roald Dahl

The Black Stallion, Walter Farley

Thor and the Giants, Anita Feagles

Great Brain books, John D. Fitzgerald

Harriet the Spy, Louise Fitzhugh

Johnny Tremain, Esther Forbes

Selections from *Poor Richard's Almanack,* Benjamin Franklin

Lincoln: A Photobiography, Russell Freedman

And Then What Happened, Paul Revere?; What's the Big Idea, Ben Franklin?; and *Where Was Patrick Henry on the 29th of May?,* Jean Fritz

A Swinger of Birches: Poems of Robert Frost for Young People, Robert Frost

Julie of the Wolves, Jean Craighead George

The Wind in the Willows, Kenneth Grahame

Mythology, Edith Hamilton

The People Could Fly: American Black Folk Tales, Virginia Hamilton

Misty of Chincoteague and *Brighty of the Grand Canyon,* Marguerite Henry

At the Top of My Voice and Other Poems, Felice Holmon

The Phantom Tollbooth, Norton Juster

The Trumpeter of Krakow, Eric Kelly

The Jungle Book and *Captains Courageous,* Rudyard Kipling

Lassie Come Home, Eric Knight

From the Mixed-Up Files of Mrs. Basil E. Frankweiler, E. L. Konigsburg

Tales from Shakespeare, Charles and Mary Lamb

The Rainbow Fairy books, Andrew Lang

A Wrinkle in Time, Madeleine L'Engle

The Lion, the Witch, and the Wardrobe, C. S. Lewis

The Call of the Wild, Jack London

Castle and *Cathedral,* David Macaulay

Sarah, Plain and Tall, Patricia MacLachlan

Paul Bunyan Swings His Axe, Dell J. McCormick

Snow Treasure, Marie McSwigan

The Borrowers, Mary Norton

Hailstones and Halibut Bones, poems by Mary O'Neill

Bridge to Terabithia and *The Great Gilly Hopkins,* Katherine Paterson

Tales of Mystery and Imagination, Edgar Allan Poe

The Merry Adventures of Robin Hood, Howard Pyle

The Westing Game, Ellen Raskin

Where the Red Fern Grows, Wilson Rawls

Bambi, Felix Salten

Abe Lincoln Grows Up and *Rootabaga Stories*, Carl Sandburg

Cricket in Times Square, George Selden

Black Beauty, Anna Sewell

A Day of Pleasure: Stories of a Boy Growing up in Warsaw, Isaac Bashevis Singer

Call It Courage, Armstrong Sperry

Heidi, Johanna Spyri

Treasure Island, Robert Louis Stevenson

American Tall-Tale Animals, Adrien Stoutenburg

The Nutcracker: A Story and a Ballet, Ellen Switzer

Swiss Family Robinson, Johann Wyss

isfactory), and if the school's course is clearly superior to the one below and even covers material for the next grade, give the school an "A" (for above average). Compare the A's, S's and F's to get a final evaluation of the curriculum for any particular grade.

FOURTH GRADE CURRICULUM

English

1. *Reading.* Two periods daily devoted to English program. Selections from classical children's literature (see Table 4). Emphasis on critical reading, with examination of character, cause-effect relationships, literary conflicts and their resolution and differences between fact and fiction. _____

2. *Writing.* At least one writing assignment daily. Complete review and mastery of grammar and application to writing. Study of compound subjects and predicates, verb tenses, sentence structure, paragraph development and proper word usage. In-depth study of etymology as aid to spelling, vocabulary development and word comprehension. Expansion of expository and creative writing skills, including use of dialogue, introductions, conclusions, summaries. Learning to construct sentences that include no more or less than the writer intends. _____

3. *Rhetoric.* Poetry recitations, recitation of own works, participation in scenes from dramatic works and oral book reports. Learning sounds and rhythms of well-spoken English. _____

4. *Library.* Daily use of library facilities to prepare written and oral reports. _____

5. *Technology.* Introduction to keyboarding and word processing. _____

Mathematics

1. *Calculation.* Mastery of addition, subtraction, multiplication and division using any combinations of two- and three-digit

numbers. Mastery of place values, ratios, rounding and approximation of whole numbers, mixed numbers, decimals, fractions, graphing linear functions, the banking process and means (averages), medians and modes. Story problems as introduction to algebra with emphasis on organization of materials, neat and accurate homework preparation, following directions and firm knowledge of basic number facts. Mastery of mental arithmetic. _____

2. *Geometry.* Symmetry and congruence; parallel and perpendicular lines; acute, right and obtuse angles; advanced characteristics of polygons. _____

3. *Technology.* Continued use of calculators and computers. _____

Social Studies

1. *History.* In-depth study of North American and American history and geography, from early settlements to Civil War. Study of French, Dutch, Spanish and English settlers, daily life in the colonies, the Declaration of Independence, the Constitutional Convention, the Louisiana Purchase and westward expansion, growth of canals and railroads and sectional differences before the Civil War. Careful development of study and research skills; presentation of historical information in essays, both for homework and on tests. At least one lengthy research paper required, along with oral report to the class by each student. Field trips to restored colonial or frontier towns; guest speakers demonstrate and teach preindustrial handcrafts, such as candle-making, pottery, quilting, forging. Study of relationships between art, literature and music to American history. _____

2. *Geography.* Careful tracing of 13 colonies, westward migratory routes and national expansion to the Pacific. _____

3. *Civics.* Functions of three branches of U.S. government, the evolution of the two-party system, constitutional issues surrounding slavery. _____

Science

1. *Scientific Method.* Explanation of "the scientific method" and experimental processes and explanation of how to maintain a required scientific notebook. All student research must be recorded in a neat, well-organized form for periodic notebook checks. _____

2. *Earth Sciences.* Rock formation, glaciers, process of erosion, creation of fossil fuels, the atmosphere and weather fore-

casting, the water cycle (rain, evaporation, clouds), the differences between meteors, asteroids and comets. Using news reports and their own observations and measurements, students set up weather station to study and monitor weather changes (precipitation, temperature, barometric pressure, humidity, wind speeds and directions, sunrise and sunset) and learn weather prediction techniques.   _____

3. *Biology.* Life cycle and behavior of social insects; important bones and muscles of human body.   _____

4. *Physics.* Heat as a form of energy; the concept of heat transfer via conduction, convection currents and radiation.   _____

Foreign Languages

Introductory Spanish or French (one only, with no credit toward high school language requirements). Emphasis on pronunciation, intonation, vocabulary building and conversation and dialogue, using simple verbs and sentences. Reading and writing of short paragraphs—"letters" to friends, for example. Study of culture of people and country, including children's games, folksongs, fairy tales and legends and simple arts and crafts.   _____

Fine Arts

1. *Music.* Music class at least twice a week, with emphasis on music literacy and performance of simple percussion or wind instrument (usually the recorder if student has no personal preference). Private instrumental lessons available. In addition, all students participate in two sessions a week of choral singing, in which they learn voice parts and principles of harmony. Frequent field trips to concerts or exposure to guest performers at school.   _____

2. *Drama and dance.* Opportunity once each semester to participate in fourth-and-fifth grade productions of a Gilbert and Sullivan operetta, a Shakespearean play or equivalent. Field trip to theater or exposure to professional touring company at school.   _____

3. *Art.* Studio art twice a week, using pencil, charcoal, chalk, pen and ink, tempera, watercolor, clay and paper. Study of printmaking. Survey of art history and examination of works of selected great painters, sculptors, architects and photographers. Emphasis on developing ability to see the essence of a subject—perspective, proportion, scale, symmetry, motion, color and light—and translate it into a drawing, paint-

ing or three-dimensional work. Frequent field trips to
museums and art exhibits. _____

FIFTH GRADE CURRICULUM
English

1. *Reading.* As in fourth grade, English classes take up two
   periods a day. Continuation of critical approach to literature, with selections of more complex works, including short
   stories, essays, plays, novels and biographies. In-depth examination of plot, characterization, conflict, dialogue and
   structure of different forms of literature. Additional works
   assigned for Christmas and spring vacations and over summer. _____
2. *Writing.* One assignment daily, emphasizing research skills,
   revision and preparation of final drafts. Written work expected to display knowledge of grammar, spelling and vocabulary. Grammar studies of inverted word order, direct
   and indirect objects, conjunctions, prepositions and prepo-
   sitional phrases. _____
3. *Rhetoric.* Recitation of poetry and of original student works;
   performance of scenes from dramatic works. Preparation and
   delivery by each student of an original talk for the class. _____

Mathematics

1. *Calculations.* Expansion of four basic disciplines to include
   negative numbers. Study of prime numbers, factors, multi-
   ples, the number line, the concept of infinity, percentages
   and ratios using manipulatives (geoboards, Cuisenaire rods,
   chip trading and pattern blocks) and representational models.
   Identification and conversion of decimals and fractions. Study
   of complex probability problems. Introduction to basic algebra—variables, linear functions, graphing. _____
2. *Geometry.* Use of protractor to measure angles; drawing,
   measurement and comparison of triangles and quadrilater-
   als. _____
3. *Technology.* Use of more complex computer software to model
   two- and three-dimensional geometric shapes. _____

Social Studies

1. *History.* American history and geography from the Civil War
   to the present. Events leading to Civil War, slavery and ab-

olition, the war itself, reconstruction, the industrial revolution, urbanization and immigration, World War I, the Great Depression and the New Deal, World War II, the Cold War, the civil rights movement, the Vietnam War, the current era. Where appropriate, local and state highlights included. Field trips to related sites or museums. _____
2. *Geography.* Memorization of the 50 states and their capitals. Map work identifies Union, border and Confederate states and traces major military campaigns and source countries of 19th century immigration. Memorization of major countries of Europe and the world and their capitals. _____

Science

1. *Life sciences.* Reproduction of plants and flowers, photosynthesis, basic structures and functions of human body, food groups and nutrition. Evolution, including development of the earth, fossils, dinosaurs, prehistoric life. _____
2. *Earth sciences.* Geological eras and changes in the earth's form; water movements; problems of pollution, conservation. _____
3. *Physics.* Complex machines and mathematical concept of work, with ties to history studies of industrial revolution. _____
4. *Research.* Keeping careful records in research notebook (learned in fourth grade), students study and examine cross-sections of plants (tree trunks, celery stems), grow mold on bread, observe mushroom spores and make spore prints on paper and study primitive plants such as algae. _____

Foreign Languages

Introductory Spanish or French. Continuation of studies in grade four to include more complex sentence structures (compound sentences, modifying phrases). Emphasis on vocabulary building, study of customs, geography of French-speaking or Spanish-speaking worlds. _____

Fine Arts

1. *Music.* Continuation of grade four program. In addition, once-a-week participation required in instrumental work for students not already taking private instruction in an instrument. To fulfill requirement, students may select any of the following band instruments: trumpet, French horn, trombone, oboe, flute, clarinet, mallet instruments or percus-

sion. Students learn fundamentals and technical skills for performance in band concert at end of year. Students may opt to study acoustic guitar instead and learn chord positions and note reading. String and piano players may participate in chamber music ensemble or orchestra. Advanced students of other instruments may also join orchestra. ____
2. *Art.* Continuation of grade four program. ____

SIXTH GRADE CURRICULUM
English

1. *Reading.* Review of reading skills acquired in fourth and fifth grades. Introduction to classical mythology and to lyric, narrative and dramatic poetry. Extension of studies of different forms of prose—the short story, essay, novel. Critical studies focus on characterization, structure, vocabulary and interpretation. Extra books assigned for vacation periods— one for each of the short vacations during the school year and three or four over the summer. ____
2. *Writing.* Vast expansion to include poetry writing and study of the effects of rhythms and imagery, essay writing, book reviews, short narratives and formal letters. Grammar studies include parts of speech, usage, irregular verbs, the subjunctive mood, punctuation, capitalization, the phrase, paragraph organization and development. Daily writing assignments hone skills in sentence structure, paragraph development, unity, transition and diction. ____
3. *Rhetoric.* Memorization and recitation of poetry. Class discussions on literary interpretation. ____

Mathematics

1. *Calculation.* Arithmetic and geometric series; the associative, commutative and distributive properties of numerical expressions; exponents, square roots and cube roots; basic functional relationships. Development of mathematical problem-solving abilities using simple equations with variables, including percentages, ratios and negative numbers. Thorough review of decimal system. ____
2. *Geometry.* Formulas for calculating length, area, volume of geometric shapes and figures; study of circles, cylinders, spheres and cones. Study of the Pythagorean theorem and

angle-sum theorem. Model construction of regular poly-
hedra.   ____
3. *Technology.* Instruction and practice in use of applicable
software for above mathematics and geometry studies.   ____

Social Studies

1. *History.* Ancient and medieval history, beginning with origins
of man and civilization; ancient Middle Eastern, Egyptian,
Greek and Roman civilizations; ancient civilizations in In-
dia᾽ and China; growth of Judaism and Christianity; the
Byzantine Empire, the Dark Ages, the rise of Islam, the
Middle Ages.   ____
2. *Geography.* Study of historical atlas and changes in world
geography with rise and fall of various empires and civilizations, sea and land trade routes that helped spread civilization and historic origins of modern countries, names of
countries and capital cities then and now.   ____
3. *Civics.* Study of the Greek city-state and relationship of original "democracy" to present-day democracy.   ____

Science

1. *Scientific Method.* Emphasis on gathering data, careful obser-
vation, neat and orderly recording of materials and logical
deductions culminating in analysis and clear presentation
of results. One long-term, independent research project due
in spring.   ____
2. *Physics.* Atomic theory of matter; states of matter (solid, liq-
uid, gas); conservation of matter; relationship of weight,
volume and density; simple optics, including reflection and
refraction of light by mirrors, lenses and prisms; study of
colors; study of boiling and freezing points of common substances, with careful record keeping and graphs. Field trip
to appropriate museum or industrial installation.   ____
3. *Geology.* Structure of the earth's crust and plate tectonics. ____
4. *Biology.* Distinctions between living and nonliving things;
instinct and learning in animals.   ____

Foreign Languages

(Note: To facilitate transfer students, middle school language courses
usually "start from scratch" and do not depend on having studied languages in fourth and fifth grades. Depending on the school district and

its definition of middle school, the following may be offered in sixth or seventh grade. If sixth grade is a part of elementary school, only a modern foreign language is offered and the contents are simply an extension of the fourth and fifth grade offering.)

1. *General Languages* (may be incorporated in English, Latin or modern language study). The study of etymology, with emphasis on Greek and Latin roots, suffixes and prefixes. History of the English language and its Greek, Latin, Norman, Germanic and Anglo-Saxon roots. _____
2. *Classical.* Beginning Latin (required at superior private schools, optional at most superior public schools, but highly recommended as base for study of foreign Romance languages and improved performance in English). Declension of nouns, conjugation of verbs, mastery of elementary vocabulary. Emphasis on word-for-word translations. _____
3. *Modern Language* (French or Spanish). Development of oral skills and verbal communication through lively listening and speaking activities, including audio and video tapes featuring native speakers in authentic situations. Simple rules of grammar and expansion of vocabulary by rote memorization. Study of geography, customs and culture of countries where the language is spoken. _____

Fine Arts

1. *Music.* Continuation of grade five program, with emphasis on performing in band or orchestra or singing in chorus. Band and orchestral work focuses on development of skills and study habits necessary for successful rehearsals and performances. Choral training includes development of sight-reading skills, ear training and techniques needed to produce unified choral sound. _____
2. *Art.* Increased emphasis on history of art, with study of masterworks to motivate studio projects. Advanced training of drawing skills by analysis of basic geometric shapes found in all objects. Study of shading techniques and perspective to transform flat shapes into implied forms. Study of contour and gesture drawing. _____

CHAPTER 9

MIDDLE SCHOOL (GRADES SEVEN AND EIGHT)

Middle school marks "a new beginning" for tens of thousands of students across the United States. For one reason or another, they find themselves in new schools and new school districts, which, whether public or private, usually give all incoming seventh graders a chance to get to the same academic "starting line" by Columbus Day. So the seventh grade curriculum will involve a great deal of review work. The more thorough the review, the better your children will do when they face the more adult-level work of high school. Unless otherwise stated, all English, math, social studies (history, geography and civics combined), foreign language and science courses meet five times weekly (40 to 50 minutes per period). Science laboratories meet two to three periods weekly apart from science classes. Music performance and studio art sessions meet three times weekly. Superior schools schedule an additional weekly writing period for writing original, graded compositions apart from assigned homework. In addition, most good middle schools schedule a once-weekly seminar on study skills for sixth, seventh or eighth graders. The first year of middle school is the most appropriate time for such a course, in which small groups of no more than eight students meet with a skilled teacher to learn methods of studying the long reading assignments they face for the first time. The techniques they learn for speed reading, outlining and organizing essays and test taking are essential to serious scholarship throughout high school and college.

Figure 5 is a broad outline of the seventh and eighth grade curriculum. Specific course descriptions follow, with a space in the margins for you to rate the quality of courses at prospective middle schools. Use the same rating system as before—"S" for satisfactory if the middle school course description is like the one below, "A" if it's above average in terms of course materials covered and "F" if the school covers less or inferior material than the courses described below.

Figure 5

Outline of a minimum acceptable curriculum for grades seven and eight in an "average" middle school.

Subject	Grades 7 and 8
English	Grade 7: Survey of Elementary Grammar and Composition Grade 8: Survey of Elementary Literary Analysis
Social Studies	Grade 7: World History from the Middle Ages to 1900 Grade 8: World Geography and Asian History/Civ.
Mathematics	*Two from among the following one-year courses:* General Math; Pre-Algebra; Algebra
Science	Grade 7: Biology Grade 8: Chemistry and Physics
Foreign Language	Formal Language Study *Two years strongly recommended*
Fine Arts	Music Appreciation and Art Appreciation *One semester of each required*
Physical Education/ Health	Physical Education and Health (strategy in team sports, gymnastics, aerobics, self-assessment for health, drug prevention education and appropriate sex education)

Source: *James Madison Elementary School, A Curriculum for American Students,* **William J. Bennett, Secretary, U.S. Department of Education.**

Unlike elementary school course catalogs, there should be nothing vague about middle school and high school course descriptions. They should spell out what students will study and what books the students will have to read. This vague description of a ninth grade English course at a Massachusetts high school, for example, is *not adequate:*

"A study of literature, vocabulary, composition and language. The student will study the short story, the novelette, a novel and modern drama. Emphasis is placed on the acquiring of basic reading and writing skills and on the composing process."

Aside from the teacher's poor syntax, the description lists no textbooks or literature readings and tells you nothing about what your child will have to study in the course, and that's usually an indication of a substandard offering. As a consumer, you have a right to know what each teacher will teach your children. The middle school years are key years—the first in which "play" and "fooling around" (as opposed to *excitement*) are eliminated from the classroom learning process and students must approach learning as eager young scholars. Remember, once again, how former U.S. Secretary of Education William J. Bennett described what parents should expect for their middle school youngsters:

> We want our students—by the end of 8th grade—to read, write, and speak clear and grammatical English and to be acquainted with the varieties and qualities of fiction and nonfiction literature. We want them to know the essential features of American and world history, the major landscapes and nations of the Earth, and the rights and obligations that belong to citizens of the United States. We want them to be proficient in arithmetic and geometry, and familiar with basic principles of algebra. We want them to have begun exploring biology, chemistry, physics, and a foreign language; to have investigated the history and practice of art and music; and to have developed the habits of health, fitness, and athletic fair play. In short, we want . . . (them) to be fully prepared for serious and challenging study in high school.

The curriculum below is designed to fulfill those goals. Accept nothing less for your children.

SEVENTH GRADE CURRICULUM

English

1. *Writing.* Thorough survey of elementary grammar and composition. Diagram sentences; review parts of speech and sentence structure; study active and passive voices, verbals (infinitives, participles, gerunds), complements, independent and subordinate clauses, compound and complex sentences. Warriner's *English Grammar and Composition* is one of several texts widely recognized as definitive references on proper English usage. Writing instruction concentrates on five-paragraph compositions, highlighting topic sentences, supporting ideas, varied sentence structure and conclusions. At least one writing assignment every day and one on weekends plus a weekly period for writing an original, graded composition on a topic unrelated to classwork.

2. *Reading.* Emphasis on analyzing and interpreting underlying meanings of literature with studies of novels, short stories, essays and Shakespearean and modern plays. Continued expansion of vocabulary. Essays and reports required daily with long analytical reports required for each of eight novels read during the school year. Required reading of one novel over Christmas vacation and three more over summer vacation with comprehensive tests given on return to

Table 5

Suggested literature for students in middle school, grades seven and eight. The list was drawn in part from a Department of Education report** and in part from lists of required reading provided by public and private schools across the United States. Starred books are required at above-average schools.

I Know Why the Caged Bird Sings, Maya Angelou
The Voyage of the Lucky Dragon, Jack Bennett
A Gathering of Days: A New England Girl's Journal, 1830–32, Joan W. Blos
The Moves Make the Man, Bruce Brooks
Alice's Adventures in Wonderland and *Through the Looking Glass*, Lewis Carroll
Neighbor Rosicky, Willa Cather
The Dark Is Rising, Susan Cooper
The Red Badge of Courage, Stephen Crane
Madame Curie, A Biography, Eve Curie
Robinson Crusoe, Daniel Defoe
I'm Nobody! Who are you?, Emily Dickinson
Adventures of Sherlock Holmes and *The Lost World*, Arthur Conan Doyle
The Count of Monte Cristo and *The Three Musketeers*, Alexandre Dumas
My Family and Other Animals, Gerald Durrell
The Fun of It: Random Records of My Own Flying and of Women in Aviation, Amelia Earhart
The Refugee Summer, Edward Fenton
Washington: The Indispensable Man, James Thomas Flexner
Diary of a Young Girl, Anne Frank
You Come Too, Robert Frost
Spin a Soft Black Song, Nikki Giovanni
A Raisin in the Sun, Lorraine Hansberry
The House of Seven Gables, Nathaniel Hawthorne
The Old Man and the Sea, Ernest Hemingway
The Gift of the Magi and Other Stories, O. Henry
Kon Tiki, Thor Heyerdahl
Legend Days, Jamake Highwater
The Odyssey, Homer

Thunder of the Gods, Dorothy Hosford
The Legend of Sleepy Hollow and *Rip Van Winkle*, Washington Irving
Story of My Life, Helen Keller
Kim, Rudyard Kipling
To Kill a Mockingbird, Harper Lee
Call of the Wild, Jack London
Good Night, Mr. Tom, Michelle Magorian
The Member of the Wedding, Carson McCullers
Mutiny on the Bounty, Charles Nordhoff and J. N. Hall
Island of the Blue Dolphins, Scott O'Dell
The Scarlet Pimpernel, Baroness Emma Orczy
The Complete Tales and Poems, Edgar Allan Poe
The Chosen, Chaim Potok
The Yearling, Marjorie Kinnan Rawlings
The Light in the Forest, Conrad Richter
The Little Prince, Antoine de Saint-Exupery
Early Moon, Carl Sandburg
The Human Comedy, William Saroyan
Shane, Jack Schaefer
Ivanhoe, Sir Walter Scott
Julius Caesar, A Midsummer Night's Dream and *Romeo and Juliet*, William Shakespeare
Sonnets, William Shakespeare
Frankenstein, Mary Shelley
Upon the Head of the Goat, Aranka Siegal
The Red Pony and *The Pearl*, John Steinbeck
The Strange Case of Dr. Jekyll and Mr. Hyde, Robert Louis Stevenson
Roll of Thunder, Hear My Cry, Mildred Taylor
Huckleberry Finn and *The Prince and the Pauper*, Mark Twain
Journey Home, Yoshiko Uchida

*The Story of Mankind, Hendrik Van Loon
20,000 Leagues Under the Sea, Mysterious Island and Around the World in Eighty Days, Jules Verne
Up from Slavery, Booker T. Washington
*The Time Machine, H. G. Wells
*Ethan Frome, Edith Wharton

The Sword in the Stone and The Once and Future King, T. H. White
*The Bridge of San Luis Rey, Thornton Wilder
The Virginian, Owen Wister
Dragonwings, Laurence Yep

**James Madison Elementary School, A Curriculum for American Students, William J. Bennett, Secretary, United States Department of Education

school. Table 5 lists the type of literature seventh and eighth graders should study at school and at home. Works marked with an asterisk are required reading at superior schools. _____

3. *Study skills* (required for all middle school students, regardless of age or grade). A one-semester, once-a-week seminar teaching techniques for handling the longer reading, writing and study assignments of middle school and high school. Students learn speed reading, underlining techniques for studying textbook assignments, outlining and organizing essays and test-taking techniques. _____

Mathematics

1. *Prealgebra.* Thorough review of mathematics and geometry. Study of rational and negative exponents, scientific notation, Euclid's algorithm, factoring of linear expressions, basic principals of formal logic. Introduction of Cartesian plane to solve problems of location and distance. Story problems involve fractions, decimals, ratios, proportions and percentages, orders of operations, linear equations and inequalities. _____

2. *Technology.* A sixth mathematics class for instruction in systematic approaches to problem solving with computers. _____

Social Studies

1. *Modern world history,* from the Middle Ages to the present. Feudal Europe, the Renaissance, the Reformation, the scientific revolution, exploration and colonialism, the Enlightenment, the French Revolution, development of the English parliamentary system, the industrial revolution, the emergence of modern European states, World War I, the defeat of Germany, the Great Depression and rise of Nazism, World

War II, the Holocaust, the Cold War, the defeat of communism. _____
2. *Geography.* National political boundaries in Europe, Asia, Africa and North, South and Central America. _____
3. *Civics.* Development of European political thought and emergence of self-determination. Influence on U.S. political system. _____

Science

1. *Biology* (life sciences). A complete survey of biology, including cells, organisms and larger life systems. Survey of plant and animal kingdoms and classification of bacteria, fungi, plants and animals. Structure of cells; functions of cellular organelles; elementary genetics; the role of DNA; embryology and fetal development; function, structure and interaction of various organ systems; major ecological systems and structure and interrelationship of communities within. _____
2. *Laboratory.* Study of materials and equipment usage, scientific reasoning, working cooperatively and sharing materials and ideas with colleagues. Observations with microscopes and simple animal dissections. _____

Foreign Languages

1. *Classical.* Etymology and Latin (see Sixth Grade Curriculum in Chapter 8) for students who have never studied either before. For those who took the sixth-grade course, Latin studies progress to include extensive drills in verb tenses and conjugations and introduction of passive voice; longer passages for translation, with study of grammatical constructions used therein; study of Roman civilization and history. _____
2. *Modern language* (French or Spanish). For first-year students, repeat sixth grade curriculum. For second-year students, a more structured study of grammar with classes conducted mostly in the foreign language. Although complex new grammar is explained in English, emphasis is on listening, speaking, reading and writing in the foreign tongue. Pronunciation practiced phonetically. Grammar studies include basic language structure, adjectives, nouns, possessive adjectives, negative and interrogative structures and idiomatic expressions. Geographic, ethnic and cultural materials integrated into studies. _____

Fine Arts

1. *Music.* Continuation of sixth grade program of participation in performing arts plus addition of formal weekly class in music appreciation—an introduction to major developments in Western music, from earliest surviving examples to present. Study of musical vocabulary and biographies of major composers. Analyses of several major works heard in recordings, school performances or concert trips. Instruction in elementary techniques of composition and instrumentation.

2. *Art.* Continuation of sixth grade program in studio arts plus weekly course in art appreciation, with introduction of major art developments from prehistoric drawings to present day. Study of art vocabularly, biographies of famous artists and principles of color mixing and composition. Detailed analyses of several major works, using films, slides or museum trips.

Eighth Grade Curriculum
English

1. *Writing.* Mastery of grammar, usage, writing mechanics, narrative and expository techniques. Daily writing assignments related to expanded reading. Emphasis on logical presentation of ideas and improved paragraph and essay structure. At least five lengthy research papers due in the course of the year. (Although this many writing assignments to correct may seem like a huge burden for English teachers, superior schools limit each teacher to three classes to give them ample time to correct assignments.)

2. *Reading.* Literary analysis of broad selection of novels, short stories, essays, plays and poetry. Classroom discussions and student essays deal with theme, plot, setting, character, mood, irony and imagery. Required readings from suggested works in Table 5.

Mathematics

1. *Algebra.* Review of mathematical concepts, probability, permutations, geometry, functions and graphing, operations with integers and rational numbers and simple equations. New

material includes equations with two variables, linear functions and their graphs, exponentials, operations with polynomials and square roots, fractional equations and inequalities and quadratic functions and their graphs. Solution of quadratic equations by factoring, completing the square and applying the quadratic formula. ____

Social Studies

1. *Asian civilizations.* Survey of three great Asian civilizations—China, Japan and India—and their histories, cultures, religions and geographies. ____
2. *World geography.* Physical and cultural characteristics of major world regions and major countries in each. Study of international boundaries, capitals and principal cities; major landforms and bodies of water; climate, weather and natural resources; transportation and communication; commerce and economy; populations, major races, languages, cultures and religions; agriculture; and politics and government. ____

Science

1. *Physical sciences* (chemistry and physics). Broad survey course to familiarize students with properties of matter, atomic structure, elementary particles, the periodic table, compounds, solutions, mixtures, Newton's first law, potential and kinetic energy, cells and batteries, electricity, motion, sound waves. ____
2. *Laboratory.* Review of the scientific method, handling equipment and maintaining neat, accurate lab notebook. Study of volume and mass, solubility, compounds, elements, atomic model of matter. Students generate simple chemical reactions, isolate substances from solutions and mixtures and measure effect of weights on the arc of a pendulum. Final exam involves taking a sludge and isolating and identifying its ingredients. ____

Foreign Languages

1. *Classical.* Required etymology, basic Latin for students with no previous background in Latin studies (see sixth grade Latin curriculum in Chapter 8). For students with one or two previous years, students may elect advanced Latin studies

involving subjective, absolute construction and other more complex elements of Latin grammar. —
2. *Modern languages* (French or Spanish). Emphasis on speaking and listening skills and development of reading and writing in foreign language. Grammar includes expanded study of adjectives, possessive adjectives, articles, object pronouns and interrogative pronouns. Study of agreement of gender, conjugation of at least 30 regular verbs and 10 irregular verbs in definite and indefinite present, future and past tenses. Vocabulary studies related to family and daily life, school, food, recreation and travel. Extensive use of audio and video tapes. —

Fine Arts

1. *Music.* Continuation of seventh grade curriculum. —
2. *Art.* Continuation of seventh grade curriculum. —

CHAPTER 10

HIGH SCHOOL (GRADES NINE THROUGH TWELVE)

The courses your children take and the grades they earn during their four years of high school will not only determine the quality of education they get, those courses and grades will also determine the quality of college or university they eventually attend. Many of the less-demanding elective courses offered in the "cafeteria" curricula of many high schools virtually doom students to substandard education and substandard colleges. Few children of 14, 15, 16 and 17 have any basis for judging what courses are best for their education. Many don't even know what foods are best for their nutrition, and it's absurd to give them a choice over their high school academic curriculum. There is no excuse for offering them substandard courses that are educationally malnutritious, such as those offered in the "general studies track." It's up to you as a parent to see that your children take courses that will nourish their education the most. Any courses that offer *less* than those listed below do not fulfill the educational requirements of the most selective U.S. colleges—most of those listed in the top two categories of *Barron's Profiles of American Colleges.*

Those colleges require four years of high school English, three years of mathematics, three years of history or social studies (including one year of American history), three years of science (including at least one laboratory science) and three years of a modern foreign language. The National Commission on Excellence in Education believes those should be the minimum standards for graduation from every American high school. "No American student," it said in its report, *A Nation at Risk,* "should graduate from high school without first completing at least four years of English and three years each of social studies, mathematics, and science." Under no circumstances, however, should these be selected from so called "general studies," which no good colleges accept in fulfillment of high school requirements. Select only those courses listed in the "academic track"—preferably honors courses.

148

In addition to the basic required curriculum, top colleges prefer but usually do not require high school students to study one year each of art and music. Such colleges also prefer that student coverage of world history be complete—that it cover the entire span from the evolution of man to present day. How that coverage is accomplished is up to the individual student and often depends on the number of courses offered and the time and method of the offering. In the idealized curriculum below (see Figure 6), each student is urged to take four years of history, but if the middle school curriculum has already covered ancient and medieval history, the student might well skip directly to modern European history. Both are offered as options in sophomore year.

Figure 6

Outline of a minimum acceptable curriculum for "average" high schools.

Subject	1st Year	2nd Year	3rd Year	4th Year
English	Grammar and Composition Literary Analysis	Grammar and Composition English Literature	Composition Literary Analysis English/Amer. Lit.	Advanced Composition World Literature
Social Studies	Anthropology Ancient History	History: Ancient/ Medieval or Modern European	American History and American Govt. The Constitution	Electives
Mathematics	Three Years Required From Among the Following Courses: Algebra I, Plane & Solid Geometry, Algebra II & Trigonometry, Statistics & Probability (1 sem.), Precalculus (1 sem.), and Calculus			Electives
Science	Three Years Required From Among the Following Courses: Astronomy/Geology, Biology, Chemistry and Physics or Principles of Technology			Electives
Foreign Language	Three Years Required in a Single Language From Among Offerings Determined by Local Jurisdictions			Electives
Physical Education/ Health	Physical Education/ Health 9	Physical Education/ Health 10	Electives	Electives
Fine Arts	Art History or Music History	Art History or Music History	Electives	Electives

English, math, history, science and language courses all meet five times weekly (50-minute periods). Laboratory consumes two periods a week. Music and art meet three periods a week each.

Fulfillment of those requirements will leave the average high school student with room for at least four and perhaps as many as ten electives for two semesters each. Nonacademic school requirements such as health education and physical education will eat up some of those electives, and your children will use up some others with such essential elective courses as keyboarding (word processing or typing) and driver education. Keyboarding is an absolute must for every student, and few students will want to miss the chance to learn how to drive. As for the remaining electives, it's wise for college-bound students to take as many as possible of the advanced courses listed under "Electives" (at the end of this chapter after "Twelfth Grade Curriculum") at the end of the required curriculum. Gifted students who test out of lower level courses or finish the required curriculum earlier than other students should also select courses from that list.

As you examine the following curriculum, remember that most of the apparently repetitive courses that your children may have studied in elementary and middle school—American history, for example—are offered in far greater depth in high school. It's true that many of the same basic facts were covered in lower level courses, but study of the details and implications of those events is far more complex in high school. So don't let your children adopt the attitude that "I already studied all of that." They definitely did not.

Remember, too, that the first month or two of many freshman high school courses review much of the work done in middle school to allow newcomers at school to catch up with the others.

In using the curriculum to evaluate high school courses, the order in which history or science courses are taken is less important than whether the school offers them at the depth described below. In English and math courses, however, that is not the case. Be certain the high school you're evaluating covers all the English and math materials below—at the right time. If, for example, a high school English department does not offer Shakespeare's less demanding plays such as *Julius Caesar* until senior year, its English curriculum is probably undemanding and inadequate. *Julius Caesar* is easily understood by 13- and 14-year-olds and is *not* an adequate substitute for the more complex *Othello* or *The Tempest*. In other words, Shakespeare's plays vary in complexity, and students in a good school should be handling increasingly complex literature every year. One other important point about literature: it's essential for your children's education that they read works such as Shakespeare's *Romeo and Juliet* or Swift's *Gulliver's Travels* as written by Shakespeare and Swift, not as *rewritten* by censors who have decided that puns and references to sexuality serve no literary purpose. Shakespeare and Swift are two of the finest writers in the history of the English language, and they knew far more about literary purposes than any censors. Your children cannot profit from cannibalized literature. So find out in advance whether they will read original works as written by the original authors.

One other thing to find out: how does the high school handle senior year? Senior year is a time of idleness for most high school seniors in the United States, because students know they need only pass their second semester courses to graduate and gain admittance to the colleges of their choice. If the schools allow it, they simply "goof off" and utterly waste one-eighth of their high school education. Good schools do not permit it. Indeed, some of the top schools will no longer graduate seniors whose second semester grade point averages fall below 10% of their first semester averages. So check to see that your children's high schools will not allow this waste of precious time.

NINTH GRADE CURRICULUM (FRESHMAN YEAR)

English

1. *Grammar and composition.* Review of the fundamentals of grammar and sentence and paragraph construction with a definitive grammar handbook such as Warriner's *English Grammar and Composition.* Continued training in rhetoric, with each student expected to prepare one original talk for the class each semester. Training in organizing thoughts logically and persuasively and committing these to paper in carefully constructed, coherent, concisely written essays.

2. *Readings and literature.* Recognition of the artistic, social and personal elements in literature, focusing on protagonists and antagonists. Reading now limited to classics with the equivalent complexity of the following:

> *The Bible* (selections from Old and New Testaments)
> Dickens, *A Tale of Two Cities*
> Hemingway, *The Old Man and the Sea*
> Homer, *The Iliad, The Odyssey*
> Lee and Lawrence, *Inherit the Wind*
> Poetry
> Salinger, *Catcher in the Rye*
> Shakespeare, *Romeo and Juliet, Julius Caesar, A Midsummer Night's Dream*

Wilder, *Our Town*
Wright, *Black Boy*   ____

Mathematics

Algebra I. Review of all mathematical functions, with emphasis on variable expressions. First half of the year covers
operations with integers and rational numbers, simple
equations, equations in two variables and linear functions
and their graphs. Second semester deals with operations with
polynomials and square roots, fractional equations and inequalities and quadratic functions and their graphs. Use of
calculators and computers.   ____

Social Studies

Anthropology and early ancient history. Evolution of the human body and brain from the earliest primate precursors.
Development and use of tools and development of agriculture. Development of human institutions, including family,
kinship, tribes and nations, marriage, religion and law. Focus on hunter-gatherer tribes, including South African
bushmen. Examination of early civilizations in Mesopota-
mia, Egypt and Central America. Field trips to museums.   ____

Science

(Only one course required for ninth grade. Either of the following may
be studied in ninth grade and the other later.)

1. *Earth sciences* (non-laboratory course). Combined geology-
   astronomy course dealing with the earth, its history and the
   geological processes (volcanoes, earthquakes, continental
   drift) that shaped it. Composition and formation of the atmosphere, oceans, rocks and minerals. Second-semester
   study of astronomy covers structure and history of universe, origin of solar system, evolution and life cycles of
   galaxies, stars, neutron stars, black holes, meteorites, comets, asteroids, quasars and pulsars, the sun. Examination of
   concept of time.   ____
2. *Biology.* The study of life and living things, beginning with
   examination of the structure of the cell, followed by study
   of unicellular and multicellular plants and animals, including man. Study of photosynthesis, respiration, cell division,

reproduction, heredity, evolution and ecological interrelationships. ____

3. *Biology laboratory* (required adjunct to biology). Gathering, recording and assessing data demonstrating material studied in classroom. ____

Foreign Languages

1. *Classical* (optional—Latin I as part of two-year sequence). Basic grammar and vocabulary needed to read classical Roman authors in Latin II and Latin III. Survey of Roman history and examination of culture and daily life in Roman empire. ____

2. *Modern language* (French, Spanish or German). All elements of language instruction: listening, speaking, reading, writing, culture and civilization. Mastery of basic vocabulary of 1,500 words and ability to converse and write about events related to daily lives. Study of agreement of gender with articles and adjectives; comparatives and superlatives; personal, interrogative and reflexive pronouns; definite and indefinite present, past and future tenses and command form for about 120 regular and irregular verbs. ____

Fine Arts

(Choose one)

1. *Music history* (3 periods a week—may be studied any year in high school). Study and analysis of representative masterpieces in Western music, beginning with early religious and secular music and running through the Renaissance, baroque, classical, romantic and postromantic periods. A look at modern music and peculiarly American forms, such as jazz. Emphasis on recognition and appreciation of various musical forms (fugue, sonata, symphony, opera). Introduction to theory of music with emphasis on composition, instrumentation, rhythm, harmony and counterpoint. ____

2. *Art history* (3 periods a week—may be taken any year in high school). Study of representative masterpieces from key periods in history of art. Attention given to Egyptian, classical Greek, Roman, Gothic, Renaissance, impressionist, postimpressionist periods. Emphasis on recognition and appreciation of elements of design in painting, sculpture and architecture and on relationship of artistic style to broad historical and cultural developments and trends. ____

TENTH GRADE CURRICULUM
(SOPHOMORE YEAR)

English

Continuing study of vocabulary and grammar, with more intensive work on composition and literature. Continued use of definitive grammar and composition handbook. Study of meaning of poems, stories and plays in relation to author and times, with emphasis on English literature. Analysis of the "human condition"—love, death, power. Authors studied at this level should include many of the following: Austen, Blake, the Brontës, Chaucer, Conrad, Dickens, Donne, George Eliot, T. S. Eliot, Hardy, Keats, Milton, Shaw, Swift and Wordsworth. A reading list of minimal complexity would include:

Brontë, *Jane Eyre*
Dickens, *Hard Times*
Golding, *Lord of the Files*
Hersey, *Hiroshima*
Maugham, *Of Human Bondage*
Melville, *Billy Budd*
Miller, *Death of a Salesman*
Orwell, *Animal Farm*
Poetry
Remarque, *All Quiet on the Western Front*
Shakespeare, *Richard III, Macbeth*
Shaw, *Saint Joan*
Shelley, *Frankenstein*
Steinbeck, *The Grapes of Wrath, Of Mice and Men*
Twain, *Huckleberry Finn*
Wharton, *Ethan Frome*

Mathematics

Geometry. Euclidean geometry, emphasizing plane geometry and such traditional topics as congruence of triangles, direct and indirect proof, circles, polygons and properties of parallelograms, rhombuses, rectangles and squares. Introduction to solid geometry, with study of surface areas and volume of simple solids and introduction to conic sections. Use of computer.

Social Studies

1. *Ancient and medieval history* (for students who did not study it in middle school). Ancient Western history from the Mycenean Greeks to the conquests of Alexander; Roman history from 509 B.C. to the barbarian conquests, with study of model Roman Republic government; European history from the Dark Ages to the early Renaissance. _____

2. *Modern European history.* Survey of political, economic, technological, cultural, aesthetic and philosophical developments from 1500 to the present. Careful examinations of the critical French, English and Russian revolutions, the Enlightenment, industrial and scientific revolutions, origins and importance of Marxism, the rise of modern Germany, World Wars I and II and the Holocaust. Emphasis is on development of understanding of background to and development of contemporary international relations. Required reading of weekly news magazine. _____

Science

Chemistry. Survey of basic chemistry. Atomic theory, structure of the atom and nuclear energy; nuclear reactions; chemical periodicity; chemical bonding; acids, bases and salts; chemical reactions, including energy changes and changes in pressure and temperature; elementary thermodynamics; balancing equations; solutions, colloids and suspensions; states of matter; reduction and oxidation; basic organic chemistry. Use of computer. _____

Foreign Languages

1. *Classical* (Optional—Latin II). Grammar, vocabulary review. Readings: *Caesar's Gallic Wars, Orations of Cicero.* _____

2. *Modern languages* (French, Spanish or German). Expansion of vocabulary to at least 4,500 words, with consequent expansion of conversational fluency and reading and writing comprehension. Introduction of more complex grammatical structures and verb tenses such as the future and conditional perfect and imperfect, the subjunctive mood, and gerunds, participles and infinitives. _____

Fine Arts

(See ninth grade curriculum for required fine arts courses.)

1. *Performing arts* (optional). Optional participation in school
   drama presentations, chamber or jazz music ensembles, orchestra, band, chorus or singing groups. Independent study. ____
2. *Studio art* (optional). Introductory or advanced instruction
   in two- and three-dimensional art, pottery or photography.
   Two-dimensional media opportunities, including pen and
   ink, pastels, charcoal, collage, tempera, watercolor, oils,
   acrylics; three-dimensional (sculpture) media include wire,
   paper, foam core, clay, wax and wood. Individual instruction and portfolio preparation for advanced students. ____

ELEVENTH GRADE CURRICULUM (JUNIOR YEAR)

English

Review of writing fundamentals, with emphasis on expository essays and long research papers. In addition to continued study of Shakespeare and English literature, focus widens
to include development of American literature and such
major influences as Puritanism, romanticism, realism, nat-
uralism. American authors will include Dickinson, Faulkner, Fitzgerald, Frost, Hawthorne, Hemingway, Irving,
Melville, Miller, O'Neill, Steinbeck, Warren, Wharton and
Whitman. Minimum level of complexity suggested in following works:

Brontë, *Wuthering Heights*
Cervantes, *Don Quixote*
Fitzgerald, *The Great Gatsby*
Hardy, *The Return of the Native*
Hawthorne, *The Scarlet Letter*
Ibsen, *A Doll's House, Hedda Gabler*
James, *The Turn of the Screw*
Joyce, *Portrait of an Artist as a Young Man*
Shakespeare, *Othello, The Tempest*
Shaw, *Major Barbara*
Solzhenitsyn, *One Day in the Life of Ivan Denisovich*

Swift, *Gulliver's Travels* (complete, uncensored)
Wilde, *The Importance of Being Earnest*   _____

Mathematics

Algebra II/trigonometry. Review essentials of Algebra I and expand into structure and theory of real numbers and the concept of function and relation, including the trigonometric, exponential and logarithmic functions; composite functions; inverse relations; coordinate geometry; algebraic and graphical solutions of linear and quadratic equations and inequalities; the quadratic formula. Elementary probability theory, including permutations and combinations. Introduction to basic statistical tools. Use of computer.   _____

Social Studies

Modern European history. See tenth grade curriculum.   _____

Science

Physics. Survey of basic physics, including classical mechanics (Newton's laws, motion, work and energy, rotational dynamics), electricity and magnetism (charge, potential, electric and magnetic fields, circuit theory, light), wave action, acoustics, optics, special relativity, quantum behavior, atomic structure and nuclear reactions. Use of computer.   _____

Foreign Languages

1. *Classical* (optional—Latin III). Reading and translation of the prose of Livy, Caesar, Cicero and Pliny and the poetry of Ovid, Catullus and Vergil.   _____
2. *Modern languages* (French, Spanish or German). Completion of grammar studies. Emphasis is on expanded readings in history and culture of the countries and literature that reinforces those studies. Entire course conducted in foreign language with students expected to converse with relative ease and fluency.   _____

Fine Arts

(See ninth grade curriculum for fine arts requirements and tenth grade curriculum for optional study opportunities in music, drama and art.)

_____

TWELFTH GRADE CURRICULUM (SENIOR YEAR)

English

Concentration on advanced composition and in-depth analysis of great world literature, with particular emphasis on the tragedy. Authors should include playwrights from ancient Greece and Rome (Sophocles, Vergil) and such English, European and Russian writers as Balzac, Brontë, Cervantes, Chekhov, Dante, Dostoevsky, Hardy, Ibsen, Mann and Shakespeare. Readings should include works with at least the equivalent complexity of the following:

Beckett, *Waiting for Godot*
Beowulf
Burgess, *A Clockwork Orange*
Conrad, *Heart of Darkness*
Dostoevsky, *Crime and Punishment*
Fielding, *Joseph Andrews*
Flaubert, *Madame Bovary*
Hemingway, *The Sun Also Rises*
Ibsen, *Ghosts, The Wild Duck*
Melville, *Moby Dick*
O'Neill, *The Hairy Ape*
Shakespeare, *Hamlet, King Lear*
Shaw, *Pygmalion*
Turgenev, *Fathers and Sons*

―――――

Mathematics

Advanced algebra and trigonometry and precalculus. Study of matrices, arithmetical and geometrical sequences, mathematical induction, the binomial theorem, theory of functions, vectors, parametric equations, polynomials and rational functions, and Fundamental Theorem of Calculus. Use of computer.

―――――

Social Studies

American History. The birth of the republic, including the American War of Independence; the writing of the Constitution and development of the U.S. governmental system, with careful study of the Federalist Papers, the Constitution and its amendments, and the political party system; the Civil War, Reconstruction and the post-Reconstruction South; industrialization and implications for politics and public policy; foreign affairs, including studies of Spanish-American War, World War II, Korea and Vietnam. _____

Science

Optional. Students may elect to take either biology or earth sciences, whichever they did not study freshman year (see ninth grade curriculum). _____

Foreign Languages

Modern languages (French, Spanish or German). Extensive reading of literature, current newspapers and other publications; extensive writing in the foreign language of reports and analyses on materials read. All classroom conversation conducted in foreign language. _____

Fine Arts

(See ninth grade curriculum for required courses and tenth grade curriculum for optional courses that should be available in music, drama, and art.)

_____

ELECTIVES

The following electives should be available to all students who have completed the curriculum requirements listed above. Advanced Placement courses are the equivalent of college freshman courses and are designed by the College Board, which offers examinations in each course. You won't have to worry about AP course content, which is prescribed and standardized by The College Board and are about the same at every school in the United States. High scores on AP exams, which are also designed by the College Board and administered by the Educational Testing Service, can often help assure admissions to the most selective colleges and universities if taken in junior year or earlier. Colleges often grant college credits to students with high AP scores and allow them to skip the equivalent college freshman courses and proceed directly to college sophomore work.

Except for AP courses, which every superior school should offer, other electives are merely suggestions of the type of advanced electives that almost any good school should offer its college-bound students who have finished the standard, required curriculum.

English

1. *Advanced Placement* (five periods weekly). Preparation for the College Board's Advanced Placement examination, "Literature and Composition." In-depth examination of literature, with critical essays based on library reading and research due at least twice weekly. One major original research paper due each term. Required reading includes many of the works from junior and senior English plus the following:
   Aeschylus, *Agamemnon, Prometheus Bound*
   Anderson, *Winesburg, Ohio*
   Bolt, *A Man for All Seasons*
   Euripides, *The Trojan Women*
   Miller, *The Crucible*
   Sophocles, *The Theban Plays*
   Shakespeare, *Henry IV, Part 1; Coriolanus*
   Selected essays   ____
2. *The 20th century short story* (two periods weekly). Reading and analysis of two to three short stories weekly by such authors as Carver, Cheever, Faulkner, Fitzgerald, Gallant, Kafka, Lawrence, Lessing, Maugham, Porter, Roth, Shaw, Warren and Welty. Two short papers due every week.   ____
3. *Seminar in creative writing* (two to three periods weekly). Students learn to keep journals for daily notations of thoughts observations, overheard dialogue and any other material that might be useful in creative writing. Weekly assignments of varying lengths, using a variety of techniques.   ____
4. *Women's literature* (two periods weekly). A study of literature by and about women and the society that shaped this literature. Analysis of the language and forms women writers have used to express their vision of the world. Readings include short stories, novels, poetry and essays.
   Chopin, *The Awakening*
   The Norton Anthology of Literature by Women
   Gilligan, *In a Different Voice*
   Huston, *Their Eyes Were Watching God*
   Morrison, *The Bluest Eye; Sula*
   Plath, *The Bell Jar*
   Woolf, *To the Lighthouse; A Room of One's Own*
   Zipes, *Don't Bet on the Prince*   ____

5. *19th century Russian literature* (two periods weekly). Examination of the works of major 19th-century Russian authors in context of Russian history and each author's life and circumstances. Required reading:
Chekhov, *The Portable Chekhov, Seven Short Novels*
Dostoevsky, *Crime and Punishment, Notes from the Underground*
Tolstoy, *Anna Karenina, The Portable Tolstoy*
Turgenev, *Fathers and Sons* _____

Mathematics

1. *Advanced placement AB* (Calculus I). Preparation for the College Board's Calculus AB Advanced Placement examination. Study covers functions, limits, differentiation, graphing, maximum/minimum problems, rate of change, integration, areas and volumes. _____
2. *Advanced placement BC* (Calculus II). Preparation for the College Board's Calculus BC Advanced Placement examination. Study includes vector functions, epsilon-delta definitions, linear approximations, L'Hopital's rule, techniques of integration, surface area, improper integrals. _____

Social Studies

1. *Advanced Placement* (American history). In-depth study of American history from the arrival of the early explorers. Reexamines in greater depth all topics covered in twelfth grade history (see twelfth grade curriculum). Preparation of analytical essays required weekly. Course designed to prepare students for the College Board's Advanced Placement examination. _____
2. *Advanced Placement* (Modern European History). Designed to prepare student for the College Board's Advanced Placement examination in modern European history, the course covers in depth all topics in eleventh grade history (see eleventh grade curriculum). _____
3. *History electives.* The following elective courses are offered at various college preparatory schools to students who have completed the regular history and social studies curriculum but want to continue their studies in history or political science. Most of the following are offered twice weekly:
   a. Afro-American history
   b. History of the Supreme Court
   c. Civil rights and prejudice

    d.   The Holocaust
    e.   History of the Vietnam War
    f.   International relations
    g.   Far Eastern history   ____

Science

1. *Advanced Placement biology.* Preparation for the College Board's Advanced Placement examinations in biology. Presupposing a basic knowledge of both biology *and* chemistry, course emphasizes modern evolutionary theory, with extensive studies of varied adaptations by different organisms for survival in their environments. Extensive study of molecular and organismic biology. ____
2. *Advanced Placement chemistry.* Preparation for the College Board's AP examination, with intensive study of atomic structure, chemical bonding, states of matter, thermodynamics, equilibria, kinetics, electro-chemistry, descriptive chemistry and laboratory techniques. ____
3. *Advanced Placement physics.* Preparation for the College Board's AP physics exam, with in-depth coverage of all material in junior physics (see eleventh grade curriculum). Material is college-level physics, however, and is designed for students planning careers in science or engineering. ____
4. *Electives.* Superior high schools allow gifted students to pursue college-level science courses at nearby colleges or to take independent studies with a qualified teacher in such areas as bacteriology, biochemistry, botany, ecology, embryology, human anatomy and physiology, inorganic or organic chemistry, neurophysiology, zoology or any other area of interest. Students may also opt to do original research projects (see "Independent studies" at the end of this chapter). From the standpoint of school evaluation, it's important to see if the school you're looking at has the facilities for and does indeed encourage this kind of work in science. ____

Foreign Languages

1. *Classical* (Advanced Placement Latin). A two-year sequence in preparation for the College Board's Advanced Placement examination in Latin. Students learn to translate with ease and analyze the styles of Vergil's *Aeneid* (Books I, II, IV and VI) and the lyric poets. ____
2. *Modern languages—Advanced Placement I* (French, Spanish or German). Preparation for the College Board's Advanced

Placement examination in modern languages. Course demands mastery of modern language, including ability to speak and understand in formal and informal conversations and express one's ideas accurately in writing as well as orally. Expansion of vocabulary to levels adequate for reading any newspaper or magazine article and contemporary literature without dependence on dictionary. _____

3. *Modern Languages—Advanced Placement II, literature* (French, Spanish or German). Concentrated review of grammar and survey of literature from the Middle Ages to modern times in preparation for the College Board's Advanced Placement test. The College Board changes its required reading lists from year to year so that students gain no advantages knowing what questions were asked on the previous year's tests. _____

4. *Modern language options.* Many good schools arrange special group or individual instruction in other modern languages such as Mandarin Chinese (the world's most widely spoken language), Russian (the fifth most widely spoken language), Hebrew, Arabic, Italian and Portuguese. _____

Fine Arts

Continuation of offerings listed in sophomore year (see tenth grade curriculum). Advanced individual work. _____

INDEPENDENT STUDIES

Almost all superior schools encourage individual students who have completed their normal curriculum to embark on some form of independent study and research under the guidance of a teacher or outside instructor, professor or authority in that subject. Students usually meet weekly with their mentor, but work is largely self-directed. Each student is expected to present a thesis, research paper, speech, working model, diarama or completed work of art at the end of the school year. Independent studies opportunities should be available in *at least* all basic areas of the high school curriculum—English, mathematics, science, social studies, foreign languages and the fine arts. In addition, any good school will encourage and help gifted students to pursue independent studies in areas not normally covered by the high school. _____

INDEX